SOLDIERS *and* WARRIORS

SOLDIERS
and
WARRIORS

Second Edition

ROGER SHARPE

The Early Volunteer Militia Of Brant County 1856-1866

TATE PUBLISHING
AND ENTERPRISES, LLC

Published by Tate Publishing & Enterprises, LLC
127 E. Trade Center Terrace | Mustang, Oklahoma 73064 USA
1.888.361.9473 | www.tatepublishing.com

Tate Publishing is committed to excellence in the publishing industry. The company reflects the philosophy established by the founders, based on Psalm 68:11,
"The Lord gave the word and great was the company of those who published it."

Cover design by Jan Sunday Quilaquil
Edited by Edward Pancoe

Published in the United States of America

ISBN: 978-1-62563-223-4
1. History / Military / Canada
2. History / Modern / 19th Century
13.03.14

FOREWORD

Proposals in a report by the Special Commission on the Restructuring of the Reserves in 1996 recommended that the number of Reserve Army (Militia) units be cut by half - from 140 to seventy.

Canada's NATO allies recognize the value of reservists, and in most cases have larger numbers of Reserves than Regulars. Our allies recognize the Reserves as the most cost-efficient component of the Army.

The cuts recommended by the Commission will be felt in many communities across Canada. The Reserves offer many young men and women the opportunity to serve their country, while pursuing a primary career, or further education. The proposed cuts represent the disappearance of jobs, money, and the public profile of the Army in communities such as Brantford and Simcoe.

The Reserves are the foundation upon which Canada maintains her ability to respond to significant emergencies. The maintenance of a strong and cost-effective Reserves is the only way Canada will continue to make a contribution to world peace while ensuring domestic security.

The Commander, Land Forces Central Area, guest speaker at the October 10, 1996 meeting of the Brant - Haldimand - Norfolk Military Institute, defined the roles of the reserves in order of priority as

a. To provide a framework for mobilization;
b. To augment and sustain the regular component of the army;
c. To serve as a link between the military and civilian communities.

"The end product of the restructuring process must be a robust and flexible Militia structure that can be defended within the context of a general purpose combat capability."

The evaluation of Militia units is to be based on the following criteria identified by the Special Commission on the Restructuring of the Reserves (SCRR):

(a) Operational Requirements
(b) Capacity to Recruit and Retain Effective Strength
(c) Capacity to Train Individually and Collectively
(d) Regular Force Support
(e) Cost Effectiveness
(f) Historical Performance and Battle Honours
(g) Footprint and Link to the Community

"The unit must be geographically located so as to serve as a link between the military and the general population. It must also enjoy the support of the community in which it functions."

The Canadian Military Heritage Museum and the Brant - Haldimand - Norfolk Military Institute were fortunate in obtaining the services of Roger Sharpe to produce this study of the early militia of Brant County. His enthusiasm and detailed research has provided a valuable footprint and link to the military history of this community for which we owe him many thanks.

It is our hope and wish that careful consideration be given by the political and military leaders of the day before embarking on their mission of reduction of the Reserves.

Edward M. Pancoe
Lieutenant-Colonel CD (ret'd)
for
Board of Directors, Canadian Military Heritage Museum and
Brant-Haldimand-Norfolk Military Institute
Brantford, Ontario, October 1998

To all

the Volunteer Militia

men and women

who have served

Brantford and Brant County

PREFACE

Special thanks and acknowledgment are extended to the National Archives of Canada, especially Mary Munk; Archives of Ontario; Directorate of History, Department of National Defence, especially Chief Historian Steven Harris; Brant County Museum and Archives; Ontario Genealogical Society, Brant County branch; Canadian Military Heritage Museum, Brantford Ontario; National Library of Canada and the Brantford, Paris, London, Hamilton, Guelph, Simcoe, Sarnia, Woodstock and Cambridge Libraries; Brantford Expositor, Paris Star, Sarnia Observer, London Free Press, Hamilton Spectator, Grand River Sachem and Guelph Mercury; Town of Paris office; City of Brantford, City Clerk's office; and, the County of Brant office. Lastly I would like to thank my editor Ed Pancoe for the many hours he has invested in this book. His technical ability is exceeded only by his love for the subject.

Roger Sharpe
Paris, Ontario
October 1998

Table of Contents

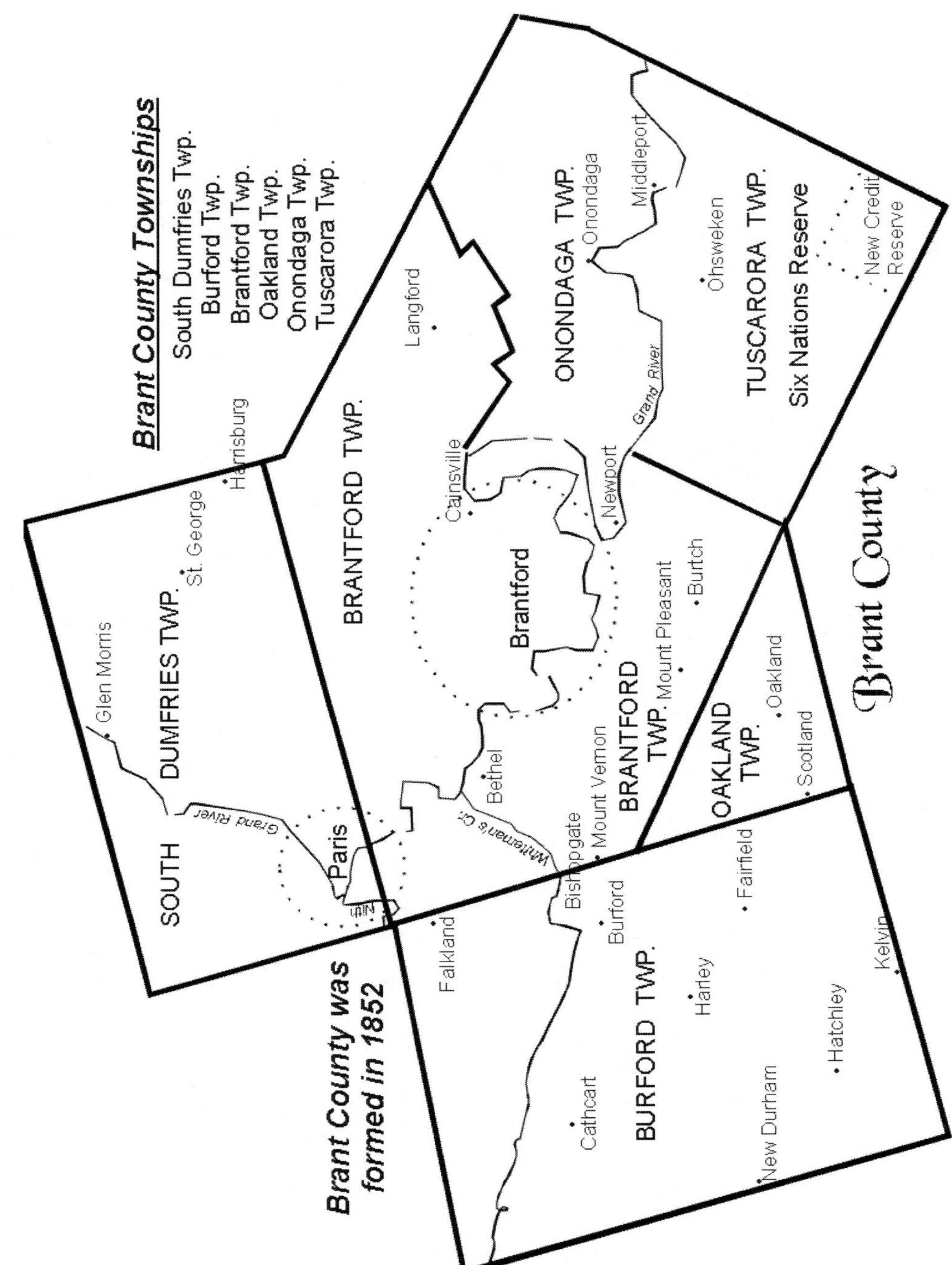

Figure 5 Map of Brant County, Ontario

Chapter 1

VOLUNTEER MILITIA BEGINNINGS

During the first ten years of the Volunteer Militia there were thirteen companies of infantry or rifles and one troop of cavalry gazetted (officially authorized) in Brant County.

In the smaller villages like Mount Vernon, Cainsville and Middleport there were units at various levels of organization but not officially gazetted by the government.[1]

Also, all throughout the county inquiries and offers of service were made by local citizens wanting to organize artillery batteries, cavalry troops or rifle companies.

Why the government didn't accept all the offers of service we don't know. What we do know is that interest continued.

It will help us to understand militia development at that time by looking at the system of militia in place prior to 1855, some of the factors occurring in Canada and abroad and some of the key figures that promoted the volunteer companies.

By virtue of his citizenship, each male between the ages of eighteen and sixty was legally required, with a few exceptions, to serve in the local unit of sedentary militia. This was a local militia enrolled in each District or County for service during emergencies. It was popularly called an 'army on paper only' because it normally paraded as a unit only once a year on the King or Queen's birthday. At this time officers would write the men's names on the annual muster roll, a few mock military manoeuvres were conducted, then the men would get down to some serious drinking. Drunkenness was commonly associated with the annual muster.[2]

In 1864 the sedentary militia roll of Upper Canada boasted 85,081 First Class, 130,553 Second Class and 54,489 Reserve for a total of 270,123 militia men.[3] This sounds quite impressive until you realize that the sedentary militia system was for mobilization of troops only, not for tactical fighting purposes.

Officers were often the most influential men of the area and were not necessarily selected because of any military experience. Because an officer can mobilize a military unit does not mean he can lead and manoeuvre his troops on the field of battle.[4]

The same is true for the rank and file militia men. Without training and practice the soldier is at a disadvantage.

This then was the sedentary militia. An untrained, unequipped and unpaid group of citizen soldiers.[5]

Britain in 1854 had become involved in the Crimean War with Russia and began withdrawing its regular troops from North America for service there. [6]

This alarmed many Canadians because of fears of war with the United States. It created a need in Canada to develop a practical defence that didn't depend as much on British regular troops.[7] Sir Allan MacNab sponsored a commission to recommend militia reform and an Efficient and economical system of public defence.[8]

This commission recommended an Active Militia of 5000 volunteers with proper proportions of infantry, artillery and cavalry. These units would be armed, equipped and paid for ten days training each year.[9]

The volunteer principle had actually been born nine years earlier in the Militia Act of 1846. At this time the government officially recognised the existence of the volunteer companies, provided it didn't cost them anything. No training, equipment or pay was provided. Actually this just regularised a situation that already existed. Groups of patriotic citizens had been organising without government support to protect homes and families, and this act formally acknowledged their existence.[10] But the volunteer militia, as a fundamental feature of Canadian defence, is normally referred to as beginning in 1855.[11]

This new system was adopted through the Militia Act of 1855[12] and within weeks the first units were enrolled. The enthusiasm was so great the government doubled the number of units the next year. In 1856 the Militia Act was amended[13] to accommodate these additional units and two classes of volunteers developed,[14] Class A and Class B.[15] The companies recruited during the first year were enrolled under Class A and received pay for their services. The only Class A company in Brant County was the Paris rifles as they had enrolled early in 1856. Class B companies that were enrolled after the first year received no pay and served more out of a desire for adventure or status. Some units supplied their own uniforms often made by a local tailor. The militia department would then supply them with arms, accoutrements, a greatcoat and drill instruction. Pay lists indicate that from 1864 on, Class B soldiers were issued pay for their service.[16]

All officers were eventually required to obtain a certificate from a Board of Military Officers[17] or a Military School of Instruction.[18] This tested their proficiency in drill and discipline. Each NCO and private was to complete ten days annual instruction and armouries were established to house government issue weapons and stores. Quite a change from the sedentary militia.

As these ideas were introduced, the character of the militia began to change, from the untrained conscripted sedentary militia, to a trained corps of volunteers.

But during the early years of the volunteer militia Canadians still relied primarily on the British regular soldiers, stationed in Canada, as their main source of defence.[19]

Also, because of the large number of soldiers required to fend off an attack by the Americans, the strategy was that only the mobilization of the Sedentary militia would provide enough troops to defeat the invader.

It was intended that the British regulars and Canadian volunteers would defend Canada, until the Sedentary militia was mobilized and ready to take to the field. In the militia departments own words, *"It must be borne in mind that the Active militia (volunteers) is but the advance guard of the army of Canada in case of a general call to arms ever should occur. The real force of the country should then be represented by the Reserve (Sedentary) Militia."*[20]

The older sedentary militia and the new volunteer militia continued along side each other for many years. But as the volunteer companies were better trained, could be mobilized in a short time and the American threat decreased, the old sedentary militia was more and more shifted to the background and was not called on again.[21] The new volunteer militia became Canada's primary militia system. The volunteer militia in Brant County began in 1856 when the men of Paris were authorized to form the first volunteer rifle company. Their history is described in chapter 3.

The next Brant County unit wasn't gazetted by the government until 1861. During the intervening years there were offers to form militia units from Brant men but none were officially accepted. Some of these offers are described in chapter 4.

In part this was due to the lack of arms for equipping any more units. It was also probably due to a desire by the government to have companies strategically located in specific parts of Canada west.

The local politicians of the area were great promoters of Brant's militia. In the early 1860s Dr. J. Y. Bown MPP for the East Riding of Brant spent time travelling around Brant County speaking to constituents encouraging them to join together and organize volunteer companies. In an 1863 news article the following is reported:

"V*olunteer Movements*

On Tuesday last Dr. J. Y. Bown MPP visited that portion of his constituency in the neighbourhood of St. George and Harrisburg with a view to calling the attention of leading men in that section of the County to the necessity of volunteer organization. His visit was not barren of results".[22]

The article continues on to describe areas where companies are being organized. It mentions that Mt. Pleasant is organized and the people of Cainsville and Middleport are organizing.

In a letter to the Finance Minister in 1863, Dr. Bown advised the minister:

"In the village of Cainsville three miles distant from Brantford is a company anxious to be gazetted. In the village of Newport, also three miles from Brantford is a company in a similar condition."[23]

Dr. Bown also tried to encourage volunteer corps development by contributing fifty dollars as an "annual contribution to the volunteers of East Brant to encourage their attention to drill and the use of arms."[24] This money was used as prizes to the men given out during competitions such as rifle shooting.

The Honourable David Christie, member of the Senate, wrote in support of both the Burford Cavalry and the Burford Infantry Company trying to get them authorized. Of the Burford Infantry Company he wrote, "they will discharge their duty to queen and country".[25]

In August 1866 the Honourable E. B. Wood MPP for the West riding of Brant wrote to the Honourable John A. Macdonald trying to influence him to authorize the Burford Cavalry Troop and Newport Infantry.[26]

The commanding officers of the old sedentary militia battalions in Brant also tried to help establish new volunteer units by using their influence to get them authorized. They made inquiries or wrote letters of recommendation for the officers of prospective units.

Lt. Col. C. S. Perley, Commanding Officer of the 5th Brant Battalion, as early as August 1856 was using his influence to try and get a Burford volunteer unit established.[27]

Figure 6 Hon. Dr. J. Y. Bown, MPP for East Brant.

Figure 7 Hon. David Christie, Senator

Lt. Col. James Wilkes, commanding officer of the 2nd Brant Battalion in 1861, unsuccessfully recommended Capt. George Racey for leadership of a troop of cavalry. He also recommended Capt. Grant's Highland Company of Brantford when they were seeking authorization.[28]

Lt. Col. A. Bunnell, commanding officer of the 1st Brant Battalion tried in 1861 to help a cavalry troop get authorized under Ensign David Curtis of his battalion. He also tried unsuccessfully recommending his Capt. G. S. Wilkes to lead a battery of artillery.[29]

Another prominent citizen who was active in volunteer organizing was Capt. William N. Alger of the 1st Brantford Rifle Company. Capt. Alger was also a Major in the Brant Sedentary Militia and was well respected. In an 1864 letter he noted, "when the government of the day decided on adding some 10,000 men to the force I visited the different villages in the County - attended several meetings - and succeeded in the formation of companies in Onondaga, Cainsville, Middleport, Newport and Mount Vernon."[30]

Figure 8 Hon. E. B. Wood, MPP for West Brant.

Figure 9 Lt. Col. C. S. Perley, first Commanding Officer of the 5th Brant Battalion.

Figure 10 Lt. Col. James Wilkes, age 92, first Commanding Officer of the 2nd Brant Sedentary Militia.

Capt. W. Grant of Brantford's Highland Volunteer Company said in an 1863 letter,

"*There are nine companies in the county ready to form into a battalion...all within an hour's march of the town.*" [31] It should be noted that only five companies were officially gazetted in Brant County at that time.

From all of this it can be seen that volunteer companies were being promoted and the people were going through the process of organizing. Some became officially recognized while others were not. Some succeeded in their organizing and some did not.

In 1871, the last of the British regular soldiers would depart from Canada leaving the volunteers to protect the world's largest undefended border.[32] Canada's militia had come of age.

So from withdrawal of British troops because of foreign wars combined with Canada's genuine concern with her southern neighbour's territorial ambitions and through the influence of Brant men, a new Canadian force called the Active or Volunteer Militia was established.

This history will cover the first ten years of the Volunteer Militia in Brant County. From 1856 when the first rifle company was organized to the reorganization of the companies into the 38th Brant Battalion of Infantry in 1866.

1. RG9 IC1, Vol. 207, #63
2. The Queen's Own Rifles of Canada 1860-1960 One Hundred Years in Canada by Lt. Col. W. T. Barnard, The Ontario Publishing Company Limited 1960 pg 2-3, and Canada's Soldiers, Stanley, pg. 209
3. RGU IIC3A3-1866, pg. 94
4. 36 Victoria, (S. P. 9) - 1873, The Annual Report on the State of the Militia
5. The Queen's Own Rifles of Canada 1860-1960 One Hundred Years in Canada, Barnard, pg. 2
6. Canada's Soldiers, Stanley, pg. 211
7. Canada's Soldiers, Stanley, pg. 211
8. A Military History of Canada, Desmond Morton, pg. 86
9. A Military History of Canada, Desmond Morton, pg. 86
10. Canada's Soldiers, Stanley, pg. 210-211

11. Canada's Soldiers, Stanley, pg. 213
12. 18 Victoria, Ch. 77 - 1855, An Act to regulate the Militia of this province and to repeal the Acts now in force for that purpose
13 19 Victoria, Ch. 44, Sec. 2, An Act to amend the Militia Law
14. Canada's Soldiers, Stanley, pg. 213
15. 26 Victoria, (S. P. 15) - 1863, The Annual Report on the State of the Militia
16. RG9 1C3, 1864 Pay lists, Vol. 10 'Brantford, Vol. 12 'Drumbo, Vol. 15 'Mount Pleasant
17. 27 Victoria (S. P. No. 13) - 1864, The Annual Report on the State of the Militia
18. 32 Victoria (S. P. No. 10) - 1869, The Annual Report on the State of the Militia
19. The Queen's Own Rifles of Canada 1860-1960 One Hundred Years in Canada, Barnard, pg. 3
20. 40 Victoria, (S. P. 7) - 1877, The Annual Report on the State of the Militia
21. The Queen's Own Rifles of Canada 1860-1960 One Hundred Years in Canada by Lt. Col. W. T. Barnard, The Ontario Publishing Company Limited 1960, pg. 4 and Canada's Soldiers, Stanley, pg. 213
22. Brantford Expositor, January 23, 1863
23. RG9 II Vol. 215 #2064
24. Brantford Expositor, May 22, 1863
25. RG9 IC1 Vol. 231 #1325 and Vol. 233 #1674
26. RG9 IC1 Vol. 235 #2190 and #2326
27. RG9 IC1 Vol. 138 #1810 and Vol. 142 #3047
28. RG9 IC1 Vol. 171 #707 and Vol. 182 #730
29. RG9 IC1 Vol. 176 #1163 and Vol. 175 #1133
30. RG9 IC1 Vol. 207 #63
31. RG9 IC1 Vol. 201 #2080
32. Canada's Soldiers, Stanley, pg. 241

Chapter 2

BRANT COUNTY AND THE FENIAN INVASION OF 1866

The Fenians

One of the early threats to Canadian sovereignty was the Fenian brotherhood who were men of Irish descent or sympathies. Their main purpose was to conquer a territory which could be used as a base of operations against the British to liberate Ireland. They openly proclaimed invasion of Canada which would be renamed "New Ireland".

The Irish leaders had been inciting others to revolt and were stockpiling weapons across the U. S. border. They had also been recruiting battle experienced soldiers from the thousands of recently released soldiers of the American civil war.[33]

Because of genuine fears of an attack by the Fenians, Canada called out its Militia.

The Call to Active Service in Brant County

At the direction of the Minister of Militia, John A. Macdonald, and the Commander in Chief, Sir John Michel, a force of 10,000 volunteers were called out for service by the following General Order. [34]

"Headquarters, Ottawa 8 March 1866

Volunteer Militia

No. 1

The Governor General and Commander in Chief directs that the following named corps be called out for service and that the said corps be immediately assembled and billeted at their respective headquarters, there to await such orders for their movement as may be directed by the Commander in Chief.

Upper Canada
(100 Companies in total)
Mount Pleasant Infantry Company
Paris Rifle Company
Brantford Rifle Companies (2)
Drumbo Infantry Company"

The first hours of the mobilization of the companies is described in the following reports.

"On the 7th March, 1866, the Adjutant General, on his way from Ottawa to Montreal, received at Kemptville, at four o'clock p.m., a telegraphic message from the Honorable the Minister of Militia, as follows:

Message.

Ottawa, March 7th, 1866.

To Colonel MacDougall.

Call out ten thousand (10,000) men of Volunteer Force. Send me by telegraph names of Corps. They must be out in twenty-four (24) hours, and for three (3) weeks to Brigade Majors and Officers Commanding such Corps as you think most desirable to be in readiness to move on your orders tomorrow.

(Signed,) John A. Macdonald

By making use of the Post Office van, the Adjutant General was enabled in the course of the journey to despatch messages and letters to the Militia Staff Officers of the several districts, prescribing the quota to be furnished in each district. On the arrival of the train in Montreal at midnight, answers were received from all the districts announcing that arrangements were in progress; and by 4 o'clock p.m. on the following day, March 8, 1866, it was reported to the Adjutant General that the total number of 10,000 men were assembled at their respective head-quarters, awaiting further orders... When the Returns were received a few days after of the strength of the Companies on service, it was found that the number called by the Governor General had been exceeded by 4,000 men; and that in place of 10,000 men, there were actually 14,000 doing duty with the Service Force."[35]

Figure 11 The steam engine "Milwaukee" was used to transport troops throughout Brant County during the Fenian raid.

All throughout Upper Canada the massive mobilization was underway.

At 11 p.m. March 7, 1866, Lt. Col. Taylor in London had received a telegram ordering him to call out 1,200 men from his district to be ready in 24 hours.

By 8 p.m. the next day, March 8, 1866, 1,245 men were mustered at the nearest railway station ready to go where they were most needed.

On the 10th, these volunteers were organized to form two Frontier Service battalions at Windsor and Sarnia with temporary reserves at London and detachments at Stratford, St. Mary's, Chatham and Paris.[36]

It was reported in the Brantford Expositor[37] that the Paris Rifle Company was telegraphed Thursday March 8 at about one a.m.. They were ordered to muster under arms and by three a.m. the whole company was in uniform parading in the streets.

Later in the morning Capt. Grant of the No. 2 Brantford Rifle Company received an order to call out his men and have them under arms in half an hour. This was done and by nine o'clock the company was assembled in the drill room. They then paraded through the streets.

Capt. Dickie of the No. 1 Brantford Rifle Company received a similar telegram and was directed to have his men under arms in two hours.

Lt. Heaton of the Mount Pleasant Volunteers received orders to muster about the same time.

Capt. Howell of the Drumbo Infantry Company received a telegram delivered by William Vanderlip, a local teamster, on March 8. He then mustered his company and hired Mr. Vanderlip and Hiram Ellis to convey them to Princeton. On March 9th they left for Woodstock. Drumbo not being a Brant County company at that time served more in support of the Oxford County companies. It is included as a Brant company because several months later it did join the new Brant County battalion. On March 10th they were ordered to Paris where they were billeted and did garrison duties as No. 4 Company Paris Detachment for about three weeks under Major Patton.

Figure 12 Canadian Volunteer Militia on Parade, 1866.

Initial Reports of the Raid

When the Fenian raid finally did come on June 1, 1866 it was reported in the Brantford Expositor as:

"Exciting News June 1, 8 a.m.

The Fenians have crossed at Buffalo and are now in possession of Fort Erie. More of them are still arriving! The troops here are ordered to be ready to march at a moment's notice. Another column is reported to have effected a crossing at or near Windsor, and to be marching on London. Let our authorities here at once organize a Home Guard of 500 men, and telegraph to the ordnance department for supplies of arms and ammunition."[38]

Figure 13 Paris junction in the 1860s. Troops were transported along the railroad lines. Six hundred militia men spent the night at Paris before proceeding to Port Colborne by rail to do battle with the Fenians.

The Galt Recorder reported:

"Fenians at other Points Toronto 5th June, 1866

A despatch from Oshawa says there is a reported landing of Fenians two miles east of here. The Horse Guard were called out and men were sent to investigate. It turned out to be a schooner lost in a fog which sent a boat ashore to ascertain their whereabouts."[39]

The London Free Press reported:

"At 12:30 Sunday morning the bugle sounded an alarm in London, and the fire bells rang, causing an intense excitement. People turned out of the churches in crowds in a state of the utmost alarm. The occasion was a report that the Fenians had landed at Sarnia and Windsor." [40]

Facts of the Raid

The facts of the Fenian invasion were not exactly as described in the articles mentioned above. The so-called invasion had petered out to a mere raid at Niagara. [41]

On Friday, June 1, a group of armed Fenians crossed the Niagara River from Buffalo and occupied Fort Erie village. As the raid advanced they encountered a group of Canadian Militia at Limestone Ridge on Saturday June 2.

The Canadian Militia units that made the initial contact with the Fenians were the Queen's Own Rifles of Toronto, the 13th Battalion of Hamilton and the York and Caledonia Rifle Companies.[42]

A battle ensued with the militia gaining the upper hand until a group of mounted Fenians came charging around a bend in the ridge road. Cavalry, which was the great dread of infantry, caused panic and because of several contradictory orders the militia were routed and retreated. This battle has become known in Canadian history as the Battle of Ridgeway.[43]

The Fenian commander, aware of the larger force advancing on him, then withdrew from the Ridgeway engagement and retreated back to Fort Erie village. A smaller secondary battle was also fought at Fort Erie. A Canadian Militia officer had taken the initiative boarding the tug W. T. Robb with the Welland Canal Field Battery and the Dunnville Naval Brigade. Disembarking from the tug at Fort Erie they engaged the retreating Fenians in a small but fierce battle. Facing an overwhelmingly superior force some militiamen retreated to the tug and escaped. Others were left to escape on their own.[44]

After a hurried embarkation, during which they abandoned their sick and many men manning outposts, the Fenians returned to the United States.

Figure 14 Canadian Militia canteen at Fort Erie, June 1866.

Defensive Strategy

Part of the military strategy during the Fenian Raids was based on use of the railways for transportation and the telegraph for communication. [45]

The rural Volunteer Companies were called out for service and ordered to report under arms to major rail depots such as Toronto, Hamilton, London and Windsor. There, during the critical times, they were billeted so as to be immediately available for transport by rail to any point under attack.[46]

Locomotives waiting with boilers fired up, were ready for immediate response, and rail cars were strategically located at these depots to convey troops in any direction needed.[47] At London station engines and cars for 550 troops were in waiting.

At the height of the Fenian scare public traffic on the rail lines was suspended and all rail resources placed at the command of the government.

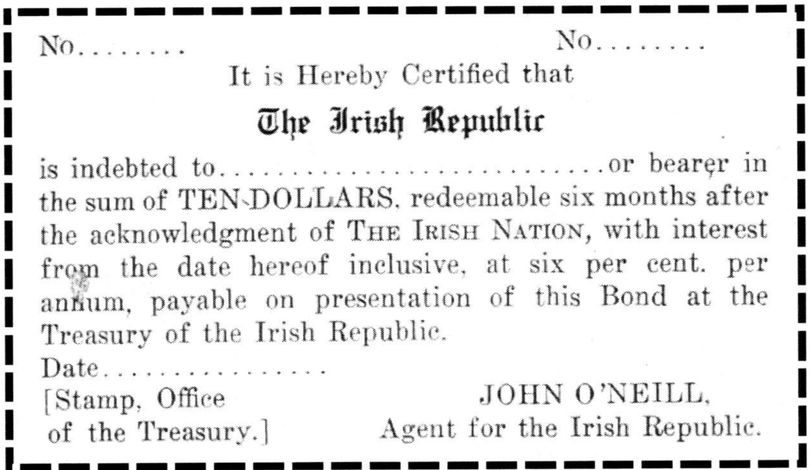

No. . . . . No. . . . .

It is Hereby Certified that

The Irish Republic

is indebted to. . . . . .or bearer in the sum of TEN DOLLARS, redeemable six months after the acknowledgment of THE IRISH NATION, with interest from the date hereof inclusive, at six per cent. per annum, payable on presentation of this Bond at the Treasury of the Irish Republic.

Date. . . . .

[Stamp, Office of the Treasury.] JOHN O'NEILL, Agent for the Irish Republic.

Figure 15 One means of raising funds to finance the Fenian raid was through the sale of bonds issued by the Irish Republic.

Bridges along the railway lines were guarded 24 hours a day. The Fenians had already burned one bridge in Niagara and loss of any of the bridges would compromise speed of troop movements.[48]

The telegraph lines were secured by not allowing telegraph companies to send any accounts of troop movements. Troops also provided physical security of the lines. [49]

Two Major Events

The Brant County volunteer companies though not directly involved in the Ridgeway battle did muster, prepare and expect to go to battle and received the 59 Fenian prisoners captured in the battle. There were two major events of significance in Brant County.

Troops to Paris

First was the excitement of over 200 militiamen gathering at Paris from the neighboring communities. Paris at that time was at the junction of the Hamilton to Windsor and Buffalo to Goderich railway lines.

A local newspaper of the time described Paris in these words:

"The way to reach the scene of action is by way of Paris. Fort Erie and Port Colborne are accessible by the Buffalo and Lake Huron Railway, which runs through Paris to the point opposite Buffalo. Paris is therefore the natural place of rendezvous."[50]

So it was of strategic advantage to have a gathering in force of troops there. Whatever direction the attack came from troops could be dispatched immediately in that direction by train.[51]

The Daily Globe reported, "*200 Men Concentrated at Paris...Orders were also received yesterday to concentrate troops at St. Catharines and Paris...*" [52]

At various times during the Fenian crisis different troops were stationed at Paris.

A detachment of troops was stationed at Paris from approximately March 8 to March 31, 1866. It was comprised of four companies:

Number 1 Company Paris Detachment was the Paris Rifle Company
Number 2 Company Paris Detachment was the Seaforth Infantry Company
Number 3 Company Paris Detachment was the Princeton Infantry Company
Number 4 Company Paris Detachment was the Drumbo Rifle Company [53]

Figure 16 Town of Paris. The railway bridge (upper right) was guarded by men of the Paris Rifle Company during the Fenian raid. Troops that were temporarily stationed at Paris were billeted in the local hotels and private homes.

These companies were billeted at hotels or private homes in Paris. They drilled daily, did garrison duties and provided security for the bridge, telegraph line and depot, which some called a reserve base. [54]

All the Brant units were released from duty on or about March 31, 1866.[55] Although we don't know how much politics may have played in the troops being released, the Hon. David Christie, a senator from Brant County did attempt to use his influence to do this in the following letter.

"Paris, 26th March /66

My Dear Blair,

I have been importuned to suggest that after the 1st April, it would be very desirable to allow the various companies of volunteers in Paris and Brantford to return to their homes. They are composed chiefly of farmers and tradesmen whose labour cannot be spared during spring work and as labourers are very scarce substitutes on the farm cannot be had at almost any price.

The men belonging to the several companies are all within 3 hours call, and should any emergency arise would at once be summoned and attend in their places.

Of course were there any real danger, this would not be asked but as things are there is no likelihood of any disturbance.

The Hon. A. I. F. Blair *I remain yours very truly,*
Woodhill *David Christie"*[56]

After the Fenian raid at Fort Erie on June 1, troop build-ups again occurred. Several companies of British Regulars stationed at London plus five London companies, two Woodstock companies, and the Princeton and Drumbo companies left for Paris shortly after 11 p.m.[57] They were unable to proceed from Paris to Ridgeway immediately and spent the night there. [58] It must have been a time of great excitement at Paris that night with 500 to 600 young men trying to sleep yet charged with adrenaline fully expecting to be engaged in a battle for Canada the following day. We can understand a little of what was going on in Paris at that time from the story of a correspondent who passed through Paris as he was making his way to Buffalo.

The following is his account:

" on arriving at Brantford I found that the eastern end of the Buffalo and Lake Huron railroad was in possession of the Fenians. The consequence was I had to lay over and proceed to Paris this morning. On my arrival there I found some five hundred brave Canadian volunteers waiting, with engine steamed up to proceed wherever their services were most needed." [59]

The troops left for the front the following day and it was reported in the Hamilton Evening Times, "*Troops Hurrying to the Front. A force of 600 Volunteers left Paris at 2 P.M. for Port Colborne...*" [60]

After the large force had left Paris it was decided that on June 2 the Mount Pleasant Company would come to Paris to provide security for a temporary reserve base and the telegraph line. [61]

The June 1st Daily Globe reported: "*At Brantford the two town companies are under arms, in command of Capt. Grant and Dickie, and at Paris two hundred men are to muster immediately.*"[62]

On June 8, 1866 all the Volunteer Companies of Norfolk County were ordered to march to Paris. There were the Fenwickes of Simcoe, the Villa Nova, Walsingham and Port Rowan companies. Accounts of the march of these troops have survived and give an excellent glimpse of the troop build-up at Paris. The Norfolk Reformer reported:

"Departure of the Fenwickes. On Friday morning last orders were received by mail instructing Capt. Tisdale to proceed with his men to Paris, and there await further orders. The order was communicated to the members of the company at ten o'clock and one o'clock was set for the time to start. The three hours intervening were marked by considerable bustle as preparations were made for the departure of our 'boys'...It was nearly two o'clock before everything was in readiness, and at that time they started on their march, headed by their brass band playing martial strains. As the men started the crowd cheered them lustily. They were escorted by a large number as far as Colborne where the men embarked in vehicles for their destination and a parting cheer was given." [63]

"The Port Rowan Company, under Capt. Mabee, and the Walsingham Centre Company, under Capt. Morgan, received orders on Friday to report to Paris and await further orders. On Saturday morning both companies started from Port Rowan for their destination. They were met a little west of Vittoria by the Vittoria brass band and escorted into the village where a substantial luncheon had been prepared for them by the citizens..." [64]

"The Villa Nova Rifles - The Villa Nova Rifle Company left home on Friday last for Paris, where they had been ordered to report for further orders." [65]

A report of the arrival of the troops in Paris was printed in the Paris Star and survived because it was reprinted in the Norfolk Reformer:

"Norfolk Volunteers

The Paris Star of last week contains the following in reference to the volunteer companies from this county, now stationed in that place:

On Friday evening last, the Simcoe Volunteer Rifle Company arrived in this town. The Company numbered about 67. One of the best brass bands we have seen for some time belong to the Company, who played as they marched into town. They are a very fine looking body of men and seem to be well up in their drill. About 10 o'clock the same evening the Norfolk No. 1 Rifle Company from Villa Nova marched into town. They are also a fine looking body of men and from their appearance we should say they would render a good account of themselves should their services be required in the field to meet the Fenians. The Company number 45 men. On Sunday afternoon the Walsingham Rifles numbering 39 men, came into town. On the same afternoon the Port Rowan Rifle Company also marched into town. They number 57 men. The two latter companies are fine looking fellows. The men are billeted in taverns and private houses, and we are much pleased to learn that there is only one opinion prevailing in town with regard to the Volunteers now stationed here - that a finer or better conducted body of men probably could not be found in any country. Major Patton is in command of the Battalion, and Lieutenant Baird acts as Adjutant. The men are drilled twice a day - once in company, and once in battalion drill." [66]

When the troops left Paris on June 21, two weeks later, they were welcomed back to their communities in the same way they were sent. Crowds greeted them, bands played, officials gave speeches and picnics were given.

Figure 17 Canadian Volunteer Militia Officers, 1866.

Fenian Prisoners to Brantford

The second exciting event that occurred in Brant County was the arrival of 59 Fenian prisoners to Brantford jail. The authorities were concerned about a second attack and they thought it best to send their prisoners further inland so they would not be liberated by the enemy in a counter-attack.

The arrival of the prisoners is described in the following account from the Guelph Mercury:

"It was after 2 a.m. of Sunday, when the precious (?) freight arrived and as it drew near the station, it was greeted with cheers mingled with hoots and yells, as if pandemonium were let loose. As the Fenian prisoners, under the guard of 30 men from St. Catharines disembarked, they were handed over to our volunteers, who were drawn up in line to receive them, and it was with the greatest difficulty that the volunteers could restrain the multitude from lynching them on the spot. Fully three thousand people lined the streets from the station to the jail, and crowded the Volunteers and their Fenian prisoners so closely that they had to halt from sheer inability to force their way through the dense masses of people, groaning and yelling, calling for "rope" and "hang them".[67]

The Dumfries Reformer noted:

"One of the prisoners made some insulting remark to the crowd, when a rush was made and the prisoners most undoubtedly would have been summarily dealt with had it not been for the exertions of those in charge. As it was, one chap drew a knife and made a rush at one of them, with the exclamation that 'he would like to kill the _ _ _ _', but he was caught just in time by the guard; and yet in another case a stone was thrown with great violence, which struck one of the prisoners on the back of the head and cut it open. But all these assaults were promptly rebuked by those in charge of the prisoners and eventually they were all safely removed to the jail." [68]

Figure 18 Brantford Jail & Court House. After the Fenian raid, 59 prisoners were held in the jail (left) until they were transported to Toronto. The 1st Brantford Rifles rented a room in the Court House (right) as an Armoury.

The prisoners stayed in Brantford jail until June 9, 1866 when they were transferred to Toronto. A continual guard was maintained on the prisoners by No. 1 and No. 2 Brantford Rifle Companies until they were transferred.[69]

It is to the credit of the Brantford militia that the prisoners were protected from the civilian mob. This very emotionally charged event was handled with the utmost of what then was called honour and what today we call professionalism. The Brant militia accounted themselves well even when the local populous was venting their rage. A rage even the militia men probably felt.

Type of Service for each Unit

At this time within Brant County there were four Companies of Volunteers organized and equipped for duty. These were the Paris, 1st and 2nd Brantford and the Mount Pleasant companies.

A Home Guard company was also speedily organized in Brantford.

Included in the contribution was the Drumbo company as it served as a loyal member of the Brant County Battalion.

The Grand Trunk Railway Rifle Companies of Brantford were organized during the mobilization and contributed to Brant's war effort.

The Six Nations warriors also didn't wait to be asked for assistance. They promptly marched to Hamilton to help.

Paris Rifle Company

The Paris Rifle Company was on active service from March 8 to June 18, 1866 at Paris. They guarded the Grand Trunk Railway bridge and drilled each day. As previously mentioned, all the bridges along the rail lines were being secured and it made sense for the Paris company to be assigned this bridge. [70]

A list of men who served in the Paris company is added in the addendum on page 97.

1st Brantford Rifle Company

The 1st Brantford Rifle Company mustered under arms from March 8 to March 31, 1866 when they were relieved from active service. They became active again on June 1 serving until July 16, 1866. [71] They received and guarded the 59 Fenian prisoners taken during the Ridgeway engagement and escorted them to Toronto on June 9. [72] On June 18 they were ordered to the front and took the train to Fort Erie. On arriving, the order was countermanded and they returned home disappointed. They had not as yet been tested in battle and sought action at the front.[73]

At the end of June they were ordered to Dunnville. On the train trip down, time was taken to stop at Caledonia so the band could entertain the residents. The Grand River Sachem noted:

"They had a fine brass band in the company under the charge of Mr. Transom, one of the best musicians in Canada, and they played a tune in excellent style on the platform, whilst the train was waiting at the station." [74]

They stayed about two weeks guarding a dam and feeder line to the Grand River that ensured an adequate water supply for the Welland Canal. [75] The canal was also an important transportation means and therefore of strategic value.

Upon their return they were met at the town station by fellow citizens and marched ceremoniously throughout the streets to town. There they toasted Her Majesty's health at several of the hotels then sat down at noon to a substantial dinner prepared by the Commercial Hotel. [76]

A list of men who served in the 1st Brantford Company is added in the addendum on page 98.

2nd Brantford Highland Rifle Company

The 2nd Highland Company assisted No. 1 Brantford Company in guarding the Fenian prisoners from June 2nd to June 9th. They also did garrison duty from March 8th to March 31st. The companies relieved from duty after the 31st had to assemble two days per week for a full drill field day. After the raid on June 1st, they were again called to active service until June 16th. [77]

From a humorous article in the local newspaper we can get an idea of what some militia men thought of their drill training:

"Drilling in the Dust

To the Editor of the Brantford Expositor.

Its not so pleasant, as the bystanders might think, drilling in the dust of the Market Square, shouldering your rifle under a broiling sun! Oh my sore feet, blistered with tramping over those vexatious little stones... Yours

A Volunteer"[78]

From a letter attached to a Fenian invasion pay list we can get an idea of the companies' working quarters.

"Since the 8th instant the hall rented by me for my own company (for which I pay $84 per year) has been used by both companies for the purpose of a Guard room and also for a drill room when the weather did not permit of drilling. Outside two stoves have been used night and day since then and gas during the night. I was obliged to rent a room for an orderly room at one dollar per week. I trust some allowance will be made." [79]

The authors suggest these quarters were probably the Kerby Hotel.

The men of the company were allowed to billet themselves meaning they might live at home.

A list of men who served in the 2nd Brantford company is added in the addendum on page 98.

Figure 19 Brantford Market Square, late 1860s. British 7th Fusiliers on parade. During the Fenian raid Brantford's volunteer companies drilled twice daily on the dusty, stony market square.

Mount Pleasant Infantry Company

The Mount Pleasant Infantry company was mobilized on March 8th and served until about June 22, 1866. [80] The March 1866 monthly pay list was signed at Mount Pleasant which may indicate they were garrisoned there but we can't be sure where March was spent. It does say that from June 2nd to June 22nd,

1866 they did special duty at Paris guarding the reserve base and the interior line (telegraph?) of communication.

A list of men who served in the Mount Pleasant company is added in the addendum on page 99.

Drumbo Infantry Company

The Drumbo Infantry Company was ordered to muster on March 8th, 1866 for active service. [81] On the 9th they left by rail to Woodstock then on to Paris where they were billeted.[82]

They were then on April 1st ordered to return to Drumbo where they remained under orders.

On June 1st when the Fenians raided Fort Erie the Drumbo company was ordered to join the contingent of troops composed of British regulars, five London companies, two companies from Woodstock and the Princeton company at Paris. [83] At Paris the troops spent the night and then moved by train to the front.

The Hamilton Evening Times reported:

"Troops Hurrying to the Front - A force of 600 Volunteers left Paris at 2 p.m. for Port Colborne. It comprises companies from Woodstock, Ingersoll and London." [84]

Accounts from Drumbo veterans could not be found. But a veteran of this contingent from London and from Woodstock recalled their movement to Fort Erie expecting to engage in battle. The Drumbo company would have had a very similar if not the same experience as described in the following accounts as the contingent of troops moved together.

The Reverend Thomas Boyd of London as a young man made the trip to Fort Erie with the London company that accompanied the Drumbo company and described the experience as follows:

"The boys were ordered to meet at the drill hall in London and when we arrived we were informed that we were to leave for Ridgeway and meet the Fenians in battle. We arrived there about midnight and slept in open cattle cars, the best we could but not many fell asleep. When day dawned we were on the march to the scene of battle, but to our bitter disappointment the battle was over, but the dead were on the field and the wounded were cared for in some old log house not far off. We followed the Fenians to Fort Erie but we found on the road traces of campfires and old clothes soaked in blood, indicating severe casualties on the part of the enemy.

When we reached Fort Erie we found the enemy had taken to their boat on the river, but were refused landing on the opposite side by United States gunboats. While we were in the little village some of the boys went in bathing but this had to be stopped on account of the firing upon them by the enemy." [85]

Mr. George Poldon who was serving at the time in No. 6 Company of the Oxford Rifles described the experience as follows:

"'The call came on June 1 and we were rushed to Woodstock in whatever vehicles were available and then loaded on a train of box cars. We were just tumbled in like sheep. We went as far as Paris and spent the night there.'

The next lap of the journey was to Port Colborne, where the men remained overnight. Accommodations were poor, many of the soldiers lacking blankets and overcoats and the food being far from appetizing he related.

By the time we reached the battlefield, the Fenians had fled and taken shelter on a scow anchored out on the river, off Fort Erie. The boys would have liked to indulge in a little rifle practice in their direction but that was forbidden' he remarked with a smile."[86]

Capt. J. Macdonald, a Fenian raid veteran, wrote a comprehensive account and mentions the Drumbo Company during the approach to Fort Erie:

"During the afternoon Capt. Akens arrived from Port Colborne with the Queen's Own Rifles, 7th Battalion of London, 4 companies of the 22nd Oxford Rifles with the Drumbo Infantry Company attached, the Caledonia Rifle Company, the Thorold Infantry Company and the St. Catharines Home Guards about 1000 men altogether. When the three columns were all assembled on the heights at Fort Erie they presented a formidable and imposing spectacle." [87]

A list of men who served during the Fenian raid is added in the addendum on page 99.

The Brantford Home Guard

On Thursday June 7 another company of Brantford men came under arms. A company of the Home Guards organized under the leadership of Captain Patterson and Sergeant Major Smith began patrolling the streets.[88] About 100 citizens had organized for the purpose of protecting property and their fellow citizens in case the volunteers were called away for duty. [89] They received their arms and accoutrements on June 7 and were patrolling the streets that very day. Henry Lemmon recalls encountering the Home Guard on June 9 in the following words.

"About 2 o'clock this morning we had the pleasure of a visit from them at our office - their rifles and bayonets glittering in the gaslight - announcing to us that they were on hand for the protection and lives of our inhabitants." [90]

Home Guard units had been organized in many towns and cities for localized protection. The Brantford unit was officially sworn in and functioned as a paramilitary unit for a short duration. Arms were provided by the government and the units were drilled like regular Militia.

A set of rules followed by Home Guard units is included in the addendum on page 108.[91]

Grand Trunk Railroad Companies

Records in the National Archives indicate members of the Grand Trunk Railroad Companies during the Fenian crisis guarded bridges and terminals, protected the Grand Trunk Railroad line and conducted Special Railway services at Erie and vicinity. [92]

First Nations people

During the Fenian crisis, as in previous times of crisis, First Nations people offered warriors to defend their and British interests.

Local and national papers ran stories of the support offered in the following articles:

Hamilton Spectator:

"The Six Nation Indians to the Rally   Ottawa, March 16

The Six Nation Indians on Grand River near Brantford have offered the service of six hundred warriors to defend the frontier, and have requested the Government to furnish rifles." [93]

The Guelph Herald:

"True and Tried. The Chief of the Six Nations, on the Grand River, has offered the services of six hundred warriors to aid in the defence against Fenian invasion, and application has been made for arms to be placed at their disposal. These faithful allies remain true to the flag as of old." [94]

From the records of the Adjutant General of Militia it's recorded that J. J. Gilkison, Superintendent of Six Nations, wrote to the Hon. John A. Macdonald, Minister of Militia, immediately after the March 8 troop mobilization. He stated , "*During the late excitement, the Indians were most anxious to be on the 'war path' and it would be well to have say 100 of them organized and equipped.*" He continued in his attempt in a letter of August 18, 1866 to the Adjutant General this time, "*suggesting the organization of 100 Indians, who, in my opinion, could be rendered a useful force, in the event of another raid from those Fenians.*" [95]

After the June 1st Fenian invasion the paper of the time reported:

"A large number of the Six Nation Indians from the Grand River are in the city endeavouring to procure arms and ammunition to take to the field in defence of their country. About 500 more are expected to arrive during the day." [96]

The local Dumfries Reformer reported:

"Brantford, Monday - Some Indians from the Indian settlement started off on their own hook today. One old fellow who fought in 1812, went to the front himself." [97]

From the information available we can't tell whether the activity is the result of one group of First Nations or more than one. But the story of a group of Delaware and Cayuga natives from the Chapel of the Delaware, on the Third Line of Six Nations reserve was fortunately preserved.

Reverend Enos Montour, a minister of that church, and a Delaware, had been educated at McGill University in Journalism.

With his ability in writing he transformed many of the First Nation stories that had, for generations been handed down in the oral tradition into a written form. [98] The story of the March of the Delaware and Cayuga to do battle with the Fenians was told to him by Delaware grandmother Jane Battice in her ninety-third year. The story describes how 50 Delaware and Cayuga natives living near the hamlet of Willow Grove decided to march to war.

At the centre of their community was the Delaware Methodist Church on the Third Line within the Six Nations reserve.

Figure 20 Chapel of the Delaware, Third Line of Tuscarora township in Brant County. After the Fenian raid of 1866, Delaware & Cayuga soldiers marched off to war from this church against the invaders.

Around June 2, 1866 the natives held a war council at the forks of the Boston and Spring creeks which was an old lacrosse field. Within their matriarchal traditions the opinion of the grandmothers of the tribe held great weight. As discussion progressed grandmother Highfly finally addressed the Council. She said that although they have prayed for peace first the path of war would have to be taken. It was decided to take what arms they had and march to Hamilton where they would volunteer to fight.

They met at the Delaware church for prayers and final words from the elders. Down the old Townsend Road the 50 volunteers walked then on to the Hamilton-Port Dover road.

A frightened Hamilton Home Guard sentry dispatched a runner when he noticed the natives coming. At the top of John Street the group was challenged.

William Monture, who spoke English well, announced that they had come to fight the Fenians.

The sergeant of the guard called his superior officer who eventually came and welcomed the native group. He finally had to advise them the Fenians had retreated. He thanked them for their patriotism then wined and dined the group with a tour of Hamilton.

They were given rations and marched back homewards. As they neared Caledonia a Home Guard sentry, Andy Murray, stood at attention as they passed. The adventure of the 1866 war was over.

This story of the Fenian invasion is still told amongst the current generation of First Nation peoples. Mr. Bart Peters, who in 1995 laid claim to being the oldest living Delaware, liked to add when he finished telling the story. "*There's another old story that goes, when the Fenians heard the Delaware were coming they packed up and went home.*"

A partial list of the native veterans of the march follows:

Anthony, Alex	John, Sam
Anthony, Mike	Monture, Alex
Burnham, Philip	Monture, William
Burnham, Jim	Moses, Cornelius
Cornelius, John	Peters, John
Dolson, Henry	Peters, Jim
Douglas, John	Smoke, Henry
Highfly, Peter	Wilson, John

The Cost of the Battle

Preserving freedom and peace often comes at a high price and in the case of the Battle of Ridgeway the cost was 10 Canadians killed and 31 wounded. The Fenian commander reported 8 killed and 15 wounded but some sources suggest the figures were higher. [99]

The secondary battle at Fort Erie resulted in 6 Canadians and 4 Fenians wounded and 3 Fenians killed.[100]

Brant County men who served during the Fenian Raid

The Addendum contains pay lists of the Brant County Militia Companies who served during the Fenian invasion on page 97. It also contains lists, by companies, of the men who applied for and received the General Service Medal for their service during the 1866 Fenian raid on page 113.

Brant County Celebrates

With the battle over and the Fenians forced from Canadian soil there were many statements of commendation for the volunteer units from men of high standing.

A general commendation was recorded in General Orders and special thanks was given to the Queen's Own Rifles for their willingness to step into harm's way.[101]

The Municipal council of Welland County presented silver commemorative medals to the men of the Welland Canal Field Battery and the Dunnville Naval Brigade. To each of the wounded the council granted 100 acres in the Cranberry marsh area. [102]

The government also eventually authorized land grants to other Fenian raid veterans. [103] Samuel Gidden of Captain Grant's Highland Rifle Company of Brantford applied for and received a grant. The location certificate authorizing his grant is added in the addendum on page 122.

When the raid excitement calmed and the troops on active service were stood down many of the communities gave large celebrations for the volunteer units. One example is the Paris celebration where 3000 people picnicked on the Grand River. The following is an account:

"Military Picnic at Paris

A grand picnic was given by the people of Paris and its vicinity on Tuesday last, to the volunteer companies stopping at that town. The weather being as fine as can be desired, nearly 3000 people assembled on the flats of the Grand River to do honor to our country's defenders. The Brantford companies, No. 1 and 2 accompanied by their excellent Brass Bands, also were on the ground; as well as the Mount Pleasant Infantry Company and the Simcoe Brass Band. The bands accompanied the stand alternately and contributed largely to the pleasures of the day. At about 3 p.m. the tables were spread with an almost endless variety of the "good things", all of which were provided by the fair portion of the assembly."

Following this was a mock military battle by the volunteers, several speeches by notable people, then games and entertainment.

"Those who surrounded the platform were, however, the old portion of the gathering, the younger preferring to stray along the river banks, or join in sports. In the evening a grand concert was

given in the Town Hall and was a very successful affair indeed. There were a large number out and the music was excellent." [104]

---

33. The Fenian Invasion of Canada West, June 1st and 2nd , 1866, pgs. 38-39 . M. Quealey
34. Militia General Order March 8, 1866
35. 29 Victoria (S. P. 4) 1866 - The Annual Report on the State of the Militia
36. 29 Victoria (S. P. 4) - 1866, The Annual Report on the State of the Militia
37. Brantford Expositor, March 9, 1866
38. Brantford Expositor, June 1, 1866
39. Galt Recorder, June 8, 1866
40. London Free Press, June 4, 1866
41. The Fenian Invasion of Canada West, F. M. Quealey; Ontario Historical Society pg. 37
42. The Year of the Fenians, D. Owen, pg 12
43. The Fenian Invasion of Canada West, F. M. Quealey, Ontario Historical Society, pg 52-55
44. The Year of the Fenians, D. Owen, pg 80-81
45. London Free Press, March 9 and June 1, 1866
46. 29 Victoria (S. P. 4) - 1866, The Annual Report on the State of the Militia and London Free Press, March 9, 1866
47. London Free Press, March 9, 1866
48. London Free Press, June 2, 1866
49. Grand River Sachem, June 20, 1866
50. London Free Press, June 2, 1866
51. London Free Press, June 2, 1866
52. The Daily Globe, June 1, 1866
53. RG9 1C3 March 1866 Monthly Pay lists, Vol. 16, files: 'Paris, 'Princeton, and Vol. 12 file 'Drumbo'
54. RG9 II A5, Princeton Vol. 4 pg. 3-5; Seaforth Vol. 4 pg. 130-131; Paris Vol. 4 pg. 87; Drumbo Vol. 4 pg. 88
55. The Spectator, April 22, 1866
56. RG9 IC1, Vol. 228, #448 (attached to #439)
57. London Public Library Scrapbook Vol. 6 pg. 73
58. London Public Library Scrapbook Vol. 1 pg. 43
59. Norfolk Reformer, June 7, 1866
60. The Hamilton Evening Times, June 2, 1866
61. RG9 II A5 Vol. 5 pg. 112
62. The Daily Globe, June 1, 1866
63. Norfolk Reformer, June 14, 1866
64. Norfolk Reformer, June 14, 1866
65. Norfolk Reformer, June 14, 1866
66. Norfolk Reformer, June 14, 1866
67. Guelph Mercury, June 7, 1866
68. Dumfries Reformer, June 6, 1866
69. RG9 II A5, Vol. 4, pg. 86 and pg 87
70. RG9 II A5 Vol. 4 pg. 87
71. RG9 II A5 Vol. 5 pg. 107 and The Hamilton Spectator April 2, 1866
72. Brantford Expositor, June 22, 1866
73. The History of the County of Brant, Warner and Beers, pg. 357
74. Grand River Sachem, June 27, 1866
75. RG9 II A5 Vol. 5 pg. 107
76. Brantford Expositor, July 20, 1866
77. RG9 II A5 Vol. 4 pg. 85
78. Brantford Expositor, June 15, 1866
79. RG9 1C3 Vol. 10 'Brantford' file, March 1866 Pay list
80. RG9 II A5 Vol. 5 pg. 112
81. RG9 II A5 Vol. 4 pg. 88
82. RG9 IC1 Vol. 228 #548
83. London Public Library Scrapbook Vol. 6 pg. 73
84. Hamilton Evening Times, June 2, 1866
85. London Public Library Scrapbook Vol. 7 pg. 22
86. London Public Library, Oxford County Scrapbook Vol. 1 pg. 43
87. Troublous Times in Canada, pg 84, John A. Macdonald
88. Brantford Courier, June 9, 1866
89. Brantford Expositor, September 8, 1866
90. Brantford Courier, June 9, 1866
91. 31 Victoria, (S. P. 35) - 1868, The Annual Report on the State of the Militia
92. RG9 II A5 Vol. 3 pgs. 169, 170, 213-216
93. Hamilton Spectator, March 17, 1866
94. Guelph Herald, March 20, 1866

95. RG9 1C1 Vol. 231 #1196 and Vol. 235 #2147
96. Toronto Daily Globe June 6, 1866: Hamilton Evening Times June 2, 1866: London Free Press June 4, 1866
97. Dumfries Reformer, June 6, 1866
98. The Feathered U.E.L., Ch. 10, pgs 49-55, Enos Monture
99. The Year of the Fenians, D. Owen, pg 80 and Troublous Times in Canada,, pg 52-53, John A. Macdonald
100. The Year of the Fenians, D. Owen, pg 81
101. Troublous Times in Canada, pg 132-133, J. A. Macdonald
102. Troublous Times in Canada, pg. 137, J. A. Macdonald
103. The Battle of Limeridge, Bertie Historical Society, June 1976, pg 15
104. Hamilton Evening Times, June 20, 1866: Brantford Expositor, June 22, 1866

Chapter 3

VOLUNTEER UNITS OF BRANT COUNTY

Paris Rifle Company

The Paris Rifle Company was gazetted (officially authorized) on June 26, 1856.[105] Prior to this George Macartney, the proposed Captain of the Paris company, had written to Col. Askin, Commander of the Militia District, inquiring about the formation of a company. Col. Askin had made inquiries about Macartney and found him to *"enjoy the very highest opinions and confidence from gentlemen of high standing".* [106] On June 6, 1856 Askin wrote to the Adjutant General of Militia recommending the formation of the company and asked Capt. Macartney to send a Service Roll (a list of proposed members) also to the Adjutant General. This roll was sent on June 16, 1856. [107]

Service Roll of the Paris Rifle Company, June 1856

Adams, Peter
Alma, Ens. Wm. Edward
Angus, Geo.
Baird, Andw.
Baird, Hugh
Barclay, Robert
Batty, C.
Begg, John
Bradford, David
Clarke, Alex E.
Clode, George
Clode, Henry
Cooper, Thos. H.
Crosbie, Andw.
Dalton, Wm.
Draper, James
Ecroyd, Thos.
Ewart, R.
Fawkes, Geo.
Finlayson, James
Fisher, James
Fonger, Wm.
Forsythe, J. C.
Gibb, Wm
Grazie, James
Hawkins, Jas.
Hazel, James
Hazel, Wm.
Howard, Wm.
Hunt, A.M.
Inksater, James
Johnstone, R. W.
Kay, John
Kirkness, John
Knectal, Danl.
Lang, John
Lee, G. C.
Loutit, James
Lowe, Robt.
Luxford, Josh
Macartney, Capt. George
McDermott, Danl.
McHaffie, John
McLean, Alex
McLean, John
McLuestron, S. B.
McNab, Stewart
Minore, John
Morton, John
Morton, Robert
Overell, Jas. C.
O'Donnell, Hugh
Patterson, Wm.
Patton, David
Patton, Lieut. William
Peirce, F.
Peirce, James
Philp, Wm.
Phippeu, S. S
Qua, Alex
Ravell, Wm.
Roseburgh, Wm.
Scott, Michael
Smith, Benj.
Smith, James
Smith, Wm.
Sturgeon, Geo.
Thompson, J. S
Thompson, James
Vanallen, John
Warnock, James
Webb, Chas
Weeks, Henry
Wright, Danl.
Wright, James

An attached letter recommended William Patton as Lieutenant and William Edward Alma as Ensign. The company was officially gazetted in General Orders June 26, 1856 as follows:

"Military District #8 Upper Canada
One volunteer militia rifle company at Paris, in the County of Brant. To be the Volunteer Militia Rifle Company of Paris. The number of privates in this company to be 63.
To be Captain: Captain George Macartney from 4th Battalion Brant
To be Lieutenant: Lieutenant and Adjutant: William Patton
To be Ensign: Ensign William Edward Alma" [108]

George Macartney was among the first group of councillors elected in Paris. Macartney was the councillor who put forward the motion to make Hiram Capron the first reeve of Paris. Paris council minutes also record him as making the motion to approve the pattern of the first Municipal Seal of Paris. He was in attendance at Quebec when the Bill incorporating Paris as a town was passed.

His professional occupation was as the second Post Master in Paris beginning about 1837. He also was involved with the Paris flour mill in the lower village.

The first evidence the author could find of Macartney's military service is when he served as an Ensign under Capt. Battersby opposite Navy Island during the Mackenzie rebellion of 1837. In 1848 he was a captain in the 5th Halton Sedentary Militia. In 1856 he took it upon himself to organize and lead the first volunteer rifle company in Brant County.

By November 5, 1856 Capt. Macartney wrote to headquarters requesting the money 163.1 pounds, [109] for their first ten days annual drill.

The company is known to have drilled in two locations. Don Smith in his history of Paris noted that the Paris Rifles drilled on the flats, [110] the level area where the Paris arena is presently located. Paris Council minutes record three times that the Town of Paris allowed the volunteers the use of the town hall for drill purposes. [111] The second floor of the town hall has a very good large room that served well for company drill. Allowing them the use of the hall was not a unanimous decision. Twice a motion was put forward to stop them using the hall but was defeated both times. We are not told the nature of the objection.[112]

By January 1857 Macartney wrote that he lost many of his men but could fill up the company in no time and that he was recruiting very selectively. [113]

From an August 16th, 1855 general order we can see the uniform to be worn by the volunteer militia rifle companies at that time.

"His excellency is pleased to direct that the colour of coats...for the rifle companies be green (and) ...be of the tunic shape such as prescribed for Her Majesty's forces. Her Majesty is content to leave the choice of the colour of the facings, of the trousers, head dress and etc. to be decided by the several companies in the manner most agreeable to themselves. Lace, if any be worn, shall be silver."[114]

Captain Macartney wrote that the Paris company had chosen Shakos as their head dress.[115]

In March 1857 the by-laws of the company were rejected by headquarters and Macartney wrote back expressing his satisfaction at the rejection. They had apparently been copied from Capt. Lymons company of Montreal and Macartney had only submitted them because the company had unanimously approved of them.[116]

The following Militia General Order identifies the kit issued to each soldier:

"Militia General Order - Adj. Gens. Office Toronto 16 May, 1856

Each volunteer in a rifle company will receive a rifle musquet with rammer, bayonet and bayonet scabbard complete, a set of rifle accoutrements consisting of a forty round pouch, pouch belt, waistbelt and gun sling, one muzzle stopper and one nipple wrench.

Each Cavalry volunteer will receive one Cavalry sword with scabbard complete, one six shooting Colt pistol, one sword belt, one Cartouche box and belt, one holster, one cleaning rod, one nipple wrench."[117]

Figure 21 Paris Town Hall - The Paris Rifles were allowed use of the hall for meetings and drill purposes. After the Fenian raid Paris council voted the town hall and the Union School and grounds for use as accommodation, free, for British regular troops.

The Canning Riot

One of the first recorded actions of the Paris Rifle Company was their "Aid to the Civil Power" on June 30, 1857. Capt. Macartney received an order at 12 noon June 30 signed by two Justices of the Peace of Oxford County. It requested the assistance of twenty-five soldiers and officers to assist the civil power which had been threatened by a group of workmen of the Buffalo and Lake Huron Railway.[118]

The company arrived around 3 p.m. at Canning finding about sixty workmen. The incident was described in the Paris Star a copy of which was preserved in the National Archives. The constable who is mentioned as injured in the article was rescued by men of the Paris Rifles when they advanced with bayonets fixed.

The following is the news article from the Paris Star:

"The Paris Star

Alarming Riot in Blenheim!
Irish Labourers Defy the Law
The Rifle Coy Called Out
Constable Nearly Killed By the Rioters
Arrests Made and Prisoners Committed

Reported for the Paris Star

The Irish labourers employed on the B & L. H. (Buffalo and Lake Huron) *Railway, and living in the Township of Blenheim, made a determined stand against performing their Statute Labour this year or commuting therefor. They defied the officers of the township and threatened them with violence. The number of these labourers in the township is considerable; they are employed in a large gravel pit at that part of the line and the land alongside of it is studded with their shanties. It was therefore felt by the authorities that the law should not be permitted to be defied by an organized gang of disorderly people; and when they found that the execution of the warrants which were issued for the apprehension of some of the culprits was opposed and the Constables threatened with personal injury if they attempted to perform their duty, it was deemed advisable to call out the nearest Rifle Company to aid the local officers.*

Accordingly a Requisition was placed in the hands of the Officer in Command of the Paris Rifle Company, by some of the magistrates of the County of Oxford; and the men were immediately called to arms, and proceeded to the spot where the men were at work whom it was desired to arrest. This was a deep cutting on the B & L. H. Railway, where gravel is excavated for the ballasting of the line. On the banks of the cutting are situated the shanties of the men employed hereabout by the Railway Company. They are quite numerous, sufficiently so to be termed a city on the 'other side of Jordan'; and when Rifle Company, Magistrates, Spectators and your Reporter came upon the scene, the population of the wild settlement turned out in all its strength like a hive of bees when alarmed. Some of the men against whom warrants were out, quickly decamped upon seeing the approaching force; the women helping them up the bank, and covering their retreat.

The Company was now drawn up on the north side of the cutting; and a person who was stated to be one of the principal servants of the Contractors was asked to step up to the Magistrates so that a quiet arrangement might be made. This he refused to do in violent and abusive language; and when the magistrates went down to him he continued his insolence in the hearing of the men. Nearly an hour was now spent in parlaying with them in the endeavour to persuade them not to force the officers of the law to use extreme measures. But no impression seemed to be made.

The men, about forty in number, were at work in the bank, and drawn up before them was a train of gravel cars, which effectually protected them from attack. Whenever any one approached within reach he was assailed with shovels full of gravel, and rough words. And the bank above the men was lined with their women, who seemed by their wild gestures and voices to incite the men to a determined resistance. A force of six Riflemen was now ordered to take their station on the gravel cars; and a dozen or so were ordered to go in and take the men against whom they had the warrants. Mr. Daniels obeyed the direction given him with more pluck than prudence. He seized one man; but no sooner had he done so than he was surrounded by several railway men, dragged down the bank, till he reached the level of the cars; then a dozen shovels were raised, and soon one fell with crushing violence upon his head. It brought him to the ground as if he were killed; and then the savages repeated their blows, with shouts, feet and fist on the prostrate, bleeding man. Mr. Thomas Allchin attempted in vain to rescue him; and finding all his expostulations unheeded, he read the Riot Act, and the Riflemen were ordered to load their pieces. Meantime poor Daniels was rescued from further violence and handed over to the care of the Surgeon of the Company. A pause of a few minutes succeeded; and the villains who were foremost in the onslaught, began to make preparations for escape. They were, however, seen, followed and captured. A panic now seized the mob; the necessary arrests were made; and the magistrates, constables and Riflemen left the scene of the tumult; followed by the choicest execrations in the Gaelic tongue. The prisoners who were fully identified as having struck the Constable were brought up before the Magistrate at Canning, and committed for trial; and the parties who were arrested for non-performance of Statute Labour, were fined for their contumacy. We are glad to hear that Mr. Daniels is recuperating. His life is not considered to be in danger." [119]

For this service the Adjutant General wrote a very flattering commendation in the Militia General Orders. It reads as follows:

"Headquarters
Militia General Orders Toronto, 23 July, 1857
His excellency the Administrator of the government and Commander in chief desires to express his thanks to Capt. Macartney and the Officers and men of the detachment of the Paris Volunteer Rifle Company who were called out in aid of the Civil Power at Canning on 30 June last for their soldierlike conduct and for the efficient manner in which they performed their duty on that occasion as requested by the Magistrates upon whose requisition they were called out, as well as by the Report of their immediate commanding officer.
de Rottenburg, Col.
Adt. General Militia"

On September 9, 1857 Macartney wrote advising of the expenses incurred during the trial of the rioters in Woodstock. He also submitted the name of John Watt for the appointment as Surgeon with the company.[120] Watt had served as assistant surgeon with the 4th Brant Sedentary Militia since June 12, 1856 and was commissioned on Sept. 24, 1857.

In November, Macartney requested that a Band Master come to Paris for a month to teach the Paris Rifle Band.[121] There is very little mention of the band from any sources. One other reference, from D. Smith's history of Paris, is a reprint of a programme for a fund raising event in 1858 which mentions "*Music by the P. V. R. Company Brass Band.*" [122]

On April 1858 Capt. Macartney wrote to Baron de Rottenburg the Adjutant General advising that he had been offered a commission in the 100th Regiment of Foot and he tendered his resignation. [123] The officer that interviewed Macartney wrote in his evaluation, "*he is duly qualified to undertake the post he seeks, that of Captain.*" [124]

On May 8th the Paris Company held a parade where Lieutenant William Patton, on behalf of the men of the company, gave an address and presented Capt. Macartney with a handsome sword as a departing gift. [125]

Macartney recommended Lieut. Patton for the Captaincy of the company and this was confirmed on May 20, 1858.[126]

William Patton was a very prominent man in the early Paris community. He was one of the first councillors of Paris. He served at various times as reeve, deputy reeve, County Warden and Justice of the Peace.

In his professional life he operated the Patton and Currey Distillery located at what is now the Lions' Park. Patton's distillery is mentioned in Smith's history of Paris. The 1867 County Directory lists him as Revenue Inspector on the Paris-Brantford tollgate road.

His military career as an officer began with a commission as Ensign in the 5th Halton followed by promotion to Lieutenant in the 4th Brant Sedentary Militia. In 1856 he was appointed Lieutenant in the Paris Rifles and accepted the Captaincy in 1858.

The Paris Rifles were inspected September 27, 1861 with 28 men and 3 officers on parade. There were 3 sick, 5 absent with leave and 3 absent without leave. The inspecting officer reported they had a very good appearance on parade and had made good progress in drill and general efficiency.[127]

We do not have any reports of the Paris company until March 1866 during the Fenian raid, described in the previous chapter, where then Major Patton is in charge of a detachment of four companies at Paris.

After the Fenian raid of 1866, the Brant County companies were formed into a unit of battalion strength and designated the 38th Brant Battalion of Infantry. William Patton of the Paris Rifles had the honour of becoming the first commanding officer of the 38th. Lieutenant Andrew Baird was recommended for the Captaincy to succeed Patton and was confirmed in the position on November 30, 1866.[128]

Andrew H. Baird was one of Paris' most public spirited and popular citizens. He came to Paris at the age of 15 and accepted employment as a clerk in Charles Whitlaw's firm. He eventually became a partner with Whitlaw and also assisted in establishing the Paris Wincey mill.

He married Cynthia Capron, daughter of Horace Capron, and lived on Grand River Street North. He was a member of the Congregational Church and was a Mason and Master of St. John's Lodge #82.

In public life he served at various times as Paris mayor, reeve, deputy reeve, Justice of the Peace and county warden. He also was a director of the Mechanics Institute, president of the Library Board and Board of Trade.

He took a keen interest in military life becoming an Ensign in the 4th Brant in 1856. When the volunteer company was established in Paris his name was on the first Service Roll. He resigned in 1869 being allowed to retain his rank of Captain.

Capt. Baird made himself known right from the beginning of his captaincy. He assumed charge just as the Paris company was gazetted into the 38th Brant Battalion in General Order Sept. 28, 1866. At this time the Paris company was numbered #3 Company with the two Brantford companies as #1 and #2 Companies. Baird took this to be an affront to the Paris company since they were the oldest company in the county. He believed they should have been gazetted as #1 Company and advised the brigade major in a letter written in October 1866.

Villiers the brigade major wrote to the district commander, "*My dear Col. Powell. For peace and quietness, gazetted this company #1 of the Brant battalion.*" [129]

On October 12, 1866 the previous was corrected by General Order saying the Paris company would be #1 "*and not as was heretofore stated in General Order #5 of the 28th September last.*" [130]

For those who may wonder who joined a rifle company of this period they can see from the following examples the occupations of some of the early militia men of Paris.

Captain William Patton	distillery operator, lived on Ayr Road
Captain Andrew H. Baird	J. M. Whitlaw & Co.
	lived on corner of Broadway & Emily
Sergeant John Kay	joiner, lived on Walnut St.
Sergeant Alex Hewson	cooper, lived on Burwell St.
Sgt. Thomas McCummin	shoemaker, lived in Upper Town
Sergeant Samuel Lee	tobacconist, lived on Burwell St.
Corporal Jas. Stevenson	cooper, boarded in the Flats
Corporal F. Tompkins	saddler, boarded at Grey's Hotel
Bugler James Warnock	carpenter and joiner, lived on River St.
Private Wm. Johnston	painter, lived on River St.
Private David Kay	machinist, lived on the Flats
Private Alex Kay	engineer, lived on Arnold St.
Private Adam Freehauf	clerk, boarded at J. Lougheed, Paris Station [131]

The history of the Paris Rifle Company continued until May 11, 1883 when it was disbanded in favour of a "City Battalion" at Brantford.[132] The addendum contains pay lists for the Paris company during 1856 to 1865 on page 99, and an officers list is added on page 109.

Figure 22 William Patton was the second Captain of the Paris Rifle Company and first Commanding Officer of the 38th Brant Battalion of Infantry.

Figure 23 Andrew H. Baird was the third Captain of the Paris Rifle Company.

1st Brantford Rifle Company

The 1st Brantford Rifle Company was gazetted on December 13, 1861.[133] Major William Norcott Alger of the 2nd Brant Battalion Sedentary Militia was elected as Captain of the company.

The first communication found is a letter from Capt. Alger to the Adj. General's office. He first thanked the government then assured them that he would allow only men of good character who would be likely to continue their residence in Brantford as members.

The next question was, 'what is the uniform and how much will it cost.' This question was central to many of the companies formed at that time. The men were often of meagre means and some simply could not join because of the cost.

The price of a uniform purchased from the militia department in 1864 can be seen on page 129.

Capt. Alger described the uniform he would choose if no order for a standard uniform was given.

"I propose adopting...a loose green or grey tunic, with black or green facings. Trousers of the same colour, full round the hips and tapering to the foot so that in winter the boot can be worn over them. The head dress to consist of a light cap with a broad horizontal peak." [134]

The answer to his question was to refer to a new dress code just issued in General Orders:

"Pattern for Clothing, Rifle Corps or Companies

Rifle Green Tunics, single breasted, with scarlet facings and black cord shoulder strap; collar and cuffs slightly braided.

Rifle green trousers with stripes of black braid on a scarlet stripe down the legs. The Highland companies (such as the future 2nd Brantford Rifles) *are recommended to wear tunics, or jackets and trews* (trousers) *the same as those used in regular service, the material and facings of the tunic or jacket to be in uniform with the other Rifle Corps."* [135]

From the Brantford Expositor we have an account of one of the first meetings trying to organize the company:

"Volunteer Corps

A meeting was held at the Pepper House on Wednesday evening last for the purpose of taking preliminary steps for the formation of one or more Volunteer Corps. M. W Pruyn, Esq. was called to the chair and A. Webster, Esq. was appointed secretary. The attendance was large. Mr. Alger explained the object of the meeting and showed the necessity of forming volunteer companies throughout the Province. He made a very impressive speech as to the qualifications of volunteers and demonstrated quite clearly that we required at least two Volunteer Corps in Brantford.

Order having been established it was moved by J. Weynes, Esq. seconded by Mr. Minore, and carried, That Messrs. Alger, Yardington and Webber be a committee to receive the names of Volunteers. About 20 names were placed upon the roll, after which the meeting was adjourned to meet again on the 6th instant in the Town Hall." [136]

On November 28, 1861 Lieutenant Colonel Wilkes wrote to the Adjutant General passing on the Service Roll of the Brantford Rifles.

"Major Wm. N. Alger of my battalion has procured the signatures of upwards of fifty men. He also recommends Robert Hearnden of this town as Lieutenant and Frederick S. Williams for Ensign. These appointments I cordially approve." [137]

The leadership had been chosen from experienced candidates as Hearnden had served in the British Army and was excellent at drill and Williams had belonged previously to a London rifle company. Also two of the men acting as Sergeants, Robert Peel and Robt. Brown had belonged to the 100th Regiment of Foot and the 14th Dragoons and were assisting with drill training.[138]

The following is the first Service Roll of the Brantford Rifles:

"We the undersigned agree to enrol ourselves as members of a rifle corps of this Town - in Class B -of the militia laws of the Province.

Brantford October 5th 1861"

Barnard, George	Harper, John	Page, James
Braund, J.	Harrison, Thomas	Peel, Robert
Brown, R. B.	Harrison, Henry	Pickering, T.
Brown, William T.	Haworth, Henry	Reburn, Malcolm
Buchanan, Alex	James, A.	Ritchie, Andrew
Burgy, Adam	Jenkins, N. J.	Rutherford, Robert
Callis, John	Kennedy, William	Ryan, Arch.
Cissin, Jacob	Lowes, Henry	Saunders, James
Clarke, Jas.	McEvry, T. W.	Schultz, Henry
Cowherd, Thos.	McGrath, William	Tutt, James

Denton, E.	McLean, Samuel	Walkinshaw, William
Dickie, Hiram	McMaster, Alexander	Webster, R. B.
Drake, W.	Miller, Alfred	Welshofer, G.
Goodson, J.	Monteith, Geo.	Wickens, A.
Gower, John	O'Brien, William	Wilkie, John R.
Gray, William H.	Page, Charles	

William N. Alger lived in Onondaga with his wife Fanny on Concession 3 west of Fairchild's Creek. He was one of the first councillors elected in 1852 to the Onondaga Council and then again to the council representing the united townships of Onondaga and Tuscarora. He was reeve of Onondaga township in 1854 and 1856 and served as a Brant County Justice of the Peace.

He was gazetted as a major in the 2nd Brant Battalion Sedentary Militia in 1856. In 1861 he organized and led the first Volunteer Rifle Company of Brantford. Then in 1865 he accepted the position as District paymaster for the Niagara area.

Noted in the Brantford town council minutes was a request from Mr. R. B. Brown for the use of the town's flags for the #1 Rifle Company. The town did allow the company use of the flags provided they were returned afterwards. [139]

On February 12, 1862 Capt. Alger again wrote submitting a more complete Service Roll and a copy of the "Articles and Regulations" as adopted and signed by the officers and men for the approval of His Excellency the Commander in Chief.

This copy of the articles and regulations is the only copy found for any of the companies but other companies would have been similar. These Articles and Regulations are added in the Addendum on page 119.[140]

The following is the February Service Roll of the company submitted to the Adjutant General: [141]

"February 1862

We, the undersigned, do hereby agree to organize into a Volunteer militia rifle company at Brantford and serve under the provisions of Class B of the existing militia law of the Province, under command of the following officers, and to uniform ourselves according to the circular letter dated Adjutant General's office, Quebec, 19th May, 1860"

Alger, Capt. W. N.	Goodson, John	O'Brien, W.
Barker, James	Gray, W. H.	Page, James
Barnard, George	Harrison, H.	Peel, Sgt. Robt.
Brown, Sgt. Robt. B.	Harrison, Thomas	Pickering, T.
Brunnel, Sgt. John	Hawatt, Henry	Reilly, Patrick T.
Buchanan, W.	Hearnden, Lieut. Robt	Ritchie, Andrew
Buchanan, Alexander	Houlding, Thomas	Ryan, Arch.
Burgy, Adam	Hunter, G.	Tutt, James
Caillon, Thos.	James, Geo. A.	Walkenshaw, W.
Callis, John	Jenkins, C. J	Watts, Alfred
Carson, Jacob	Lowes, Henry	Watty, Bugler Henry S.
Claille, Jas. F.	Lowes, John	Webster, R. B.
Clifford, Daniel	Mc allum, William	Weightman, Charles
Cook, Frank H.	McKenney, Thomas	Welshofer, G.
Cowherd, Thomas[142] [143]	McLean, Saml.	Westrop, R. R.
Denton, Cpl. E.	Miller, Alfred	Whitaker, Thomas
Dickie, Hiram	Miller, Charles	Wickens, A.
Drake, Wm.	Monteith, Cpl. Geo.	Wilkie, J. R.
Flanagan, Martin	Needham, Edward	Williams, Ens. Fred
Fry, Joseph C.	Nixon, S.	Wilson, J.

In February nearly all the men had paid for their uniforms and the tailor was engaged in making them. Alger was anxious to be inspected and receive the rifles and accoutrements (accessories) for the company.

The company was inspected by Lt. Col. MacDougall around the beginning of March with the following report to the Adj. General' s office.

"I inspected the 1st Volunteer Rifle Company of Brantford...present on parade 1 Capt., 2 Subalterns and 46 Non Commissioned officers and men all in uniform except two men...The company is principally composed of mechanics, a good description of men, and make a good appearance on parade. They performed a number of company movements in a very correct, steady and soldier like manner...He (Alger) has procured a room in the Court House for an Armoury sufficient for the safekeeping of the Arms, accoutrements and Great coats. I beg therefore to recommend that sixty rifles with accoutrements and sixty Great coats may be issued for the use of the company. Four of the rifles should be short Enfields with sword bayonets and accoutrements for the use of the sergeants." [144]

By July the company was experiencing a problem with their kit which they complained about to Capt. Alger. The complaint was about the white belts they wore with the uniform. The men were finding it difficult to keep the belts clean. It had become a big problem and Capt. Alger was concerned the men might start absenting themselves from drill practice because they didn't have their kit in order. Permission was therefore requested to blacken the belts which was given. [145]

On August 19th the Drill Sergeant sent by the Adjutant General reported to Capt. Alger. Sergeant Chissom of the Coldstream Guards was sent for the purpose of instructing the Volunteer Corps of Brantford, Paris, Woodstock and Embro. Capt. Alger had made arrangements for the Sergeant to board at the Brant Hotel for fifty cents per day. [146]

From the Brantford Expositor we find the first example of an event put on by the 1st Brant Rifles when a 'Military Ball' was advertised. It was to be held in the Kerby Hotel for the benefit of the company but the people of Brantford were also invited. Held on January 27th, 1863 it was advertised as one of the best ever to be given in Brantford. [147]

In a correspondence on September 19, 1864 it was noted that a change of leadership occurred. Ensign Hiram Dickie wrote to the Adjutant General that he had taken charge of the company six months prior by the unanimous invitation of both officers and men.[148] Captain Alger had been promoted to the post of Paymaster for the Central Administrative Battalion. Ensign Dickie's promotion was recognized in the following General Order.

"Headquarters, Quebec,
5 January, 1865

Volunteer Militia General Order

No. 1 Rifle Company Brantford

To be Captain:
Ensign H. Dickie vice Alger appointed Pay Master to the Central Administrative Battalion.

By Command of
W. Powell, Lt. Col.
Deputy Adjutant General" [149]

Ensign Dickie upon assuming charge released twenty members of whom he did not approve making the roll of the company twenty-seven. He stated his reason for doing this as wanting to get a better class of men. Since then the roll of members climbed to fifty-five. [150]

Figure 24 Hiram Dickie was the first Lieutenant of the 1st Brantford Rifle Company and the first major of the newly formed 38th Brant Battalion of Infantry eventually becoming C. O. of the battalion in 1881.

Hiram Dickie was a native of New Brunswick. His father Hector served as an ensign in New Brunswick during the War of 1812. Hiram was a farmer in Brantford township about 2 miles north of the city on the banks of the Grand River.

It is said that in 1883 he had in his possession the rifle that had belonged to Joseph Brant. He was commissioned as Ensign in 1863 in the 1st Brantford Rifles and eventually rose to command the 38th Brant Battalion (Dufferin Rifles) in 1881. Hiram Dickie was the first Lieutenant of the 1st Brantford Rifle Company and the first Major of the newly formed 38th Brant Battalion of Infantry.

In late 1865 Captain Dickie and others were soliciting funds to establish the first military band of Brantford. The article in the Brantford Expositor reads as follows:

"New Brass Band"

"Through the indefatigable energy of Capt. Dickie, assisted by others, and the liberality of our townspeople a magnificent set of brass instruments, consisting of twelve Sax Horns, has been procured with two drums as an accompaniment and a Band organized in connection with the 1st Brant Rifle Company consisting of fourteen players under the leadership of Mr. Transom, assisted by Band Sergeant Harrison.

Of the members of the band ten are experienced musicians, and therefore, Brantford, will be able, in a short time, to boast of one of the finest bands in the province". [151]

From this point the band was usually found with the company. At concerts at the Kerby Hall or Alexandra Park or on inspections such as January 5, 1866,

"No. 1 Rifle Company band accompanied the volunteers and executed various suitable pieces of music with great artistic skill and effect". They also accompanied No. 1 Company to Dunnville during the Fenian crisis playing at stops along the way. [152]

Figure 25 In 1861 the Commercial Hotel, then called the Pepper House, was used for the first meeting of the 1st Brantford Rifles. During the 1866 Fenian Raid, when the company returned from their tour of duty at Dunnville, they were given a substantial meal here.

The company's contribution during the Fenian crisis is described in detail in Chapter 2.

For an example of what type of men joined a volunteer rifle company several of the 1st Brantford men are listed with occupations.:

Capt. H. Dickie	farmer
Sgt. Joseph Pickering	builder
Private Wm. Pierce	cabinet maker and undertaker
Private Robert Welch	proprietor of Ker's Music Hall
Private Robert Heatley	professor of music
Sgt. Thomas Harrison	machinist
Cpl. Robert Westrop	baker
Private John Gray	labourer
Lieut. David Curtis	collector of Customs

Several pay lists are contained in the Addendum on page 103 and a list of officers on page 109

.

2nd Brantford, Highland, Rifle Company

The 2nd Brantford, Highland, Rifle Company was officially gazetted on July 3, 1862.[153]

Prior to that date a meeting was held to elect officers on November 26, 1861 and an account was presented in the local newspaper.

"On November 26, 1861 a meeting was held at the Kerby House for the purpose of raising and organizing a volunteer militia company. There were a large number of townspeople present at the meeting which was a most enthusiastic one, and organization was at once proceeded with, the election of officers resulting as follows:

Captain	*William Grant*
Lieutenant	*J. J. Inglis*
Ensign	*M. X. Carr*

At a subsequent meeting, held on December 3, the by-laws of the company were approved of, and afterwards sanctioned by the Department of Militia. At this meeting the non-commissioned officers were appointed, the captain appointing the first sergeant and the company the others as follows:

First Sergeant	*John McHaffie*
Second Sergeant	*Wm. O'Brien*
First Corporal	*Robert Russell*
Second Corporal	*Peter McIntyre"* [154]

Figure 26 The first meeting of the 2nd Brantford, Highland, Rifle Company was held at the Kerby House. The dining hall was used as a drill room where, fully equipped, the unit waited for orders following the Fenian raid of 1866.

On December 23, 1861 Lieutenant-Colonel J. Wilkes wrote to the Adjutant General submitting the Service Roll of the Highland Rifle Company and recommended that the company be authorized. The letter and service roll are as follows:

"Brantford December 23, 1861
Sir
At the request of William Grant, Esq. I enclose a list of signatures of persons who wish to form a Highland rifle company for the County of Brant, the headquarters will be this town.
The greater part of the company have been drilling for some weeks and have made good progress.
Should the company be organized the following are recommended as the officers.

William Grant, Esq.	*Captain*
Joseph James Inglis, Gent	*Lieutenant*
Matthew Xavier Carr	*Ensign*

These names are in the list and have the full confidence of the men. I am acquainted with them and have much pleasure in forwarding the recommendation.

I have the honor to be
Sir
Your Obt. Servant

Lt. Col. A. DeSalaberry	*J. Wilkes*
D. A. Gen. Militia	*Lt. Col. 2nd Battalion*
Quebec	*Militia*[155]

1st Service roll of #2 Brantford, Highland, Rifle Company

We the undersigned agree to enrol ourselves as members of a Highland rifle corps of the County of Brant in Class B of the militia law of the province."

Austin, Alex	Grierson, James	McLenon, James
Blyth, Thomas	Hardie, Thomas	McNaughton, James
Braddick, John B.	Hardie, John	Nichol, William
Callie, William	Henry, John	Nicholson, Archibald
Campbell, George	Inglis, J. J.	Nicol, James F.
Carlyle, John	Johnstone, B.	O'Brien, W.
Carlyle, Thomas	Laird, George G.	Park, Robert Junr.
Carr, M. X.	Marshall, George	Rufah, Robert
Cron, Arch.	Mason, John	Rutherford, James
Fair, George	McCaulay, Phillip	Tainsh, John
Fraser, Wm.	McFarlane, R.	Turner, James
Frazer, D.	McFee, John	Turner, Robert
Gardner, John	McHaffie, John	Walker, Charles
Gibson, Alex	McIntosh, Geo.	Watson, L. B
Gibson, Walter	McIntyre, Angus	Watt, Robert
Grant, Robert	McIntyre, Peter	Webster, Alexander
Grant, Wm.	McKay, J.	Wilson, Stephen
Grierson, George	McKenzie, Alexander	

William Grant was very active in the Brantford community. He was a member of one of Brantford's fire companies eventually becoming its Captain. He was also Vice-President of the Brantford Horticultural Society.

In business he was a merchant and manufacturer of men's clothing. In 1867 his shop located on Colborne Street was called Taylor and Grant.

In the late 1800s he opened a dry goods and millinery shop in St. George in the old Stanton and Ewarts building but only stayed a few months.

Joseph James Inglis was active in the Brantford community serving as a councillor in 1861. He was also a member of one of the volunteer fire companies. During the visit of Prince Arthur he served by doing crowd control. There is a humorous story of how he dressed in the Highland regalia of his rifle company with a piper and stood in a shop window on Colborne Street playing for the royal visitor. He was on the committee of the Caledonian Society eventually becoming chief of the Society. He was also a member of the Grand River Division #68 of the Sons of Temperance organization. By profession he was a clothier and tailor working on Colborne Street in the 1860s and residing at 113 Charlotte Street.

On January 15, 1862 Lt. Col. Wilkes wrote to the Adjutant General at Capt. Grant's request. He stated that twenty more men had joined the company and were making arrangements for their uniform but were waiting for the company to be authorized.[156]

William Grant's partner was going to England on business and would be purchasing the cloth for their uniforms if they were assured that the company would be authorized. He respectfully asked if the company would be gazetted and mentioned that the company met regularly for drill.

The proposed Ensign of the company, M. X. Carr, also wrote to authorities stating that it was "*Some two months since the 'Scotch men' of this place organized themselves into a 'Highland Rifle Company'*". He also stated that they had funds amounting to $400 and that a merchant in Brantford would be going to Scotland to purchase their uniforms, asked about the status of the company and the cause of the delay. [157]

Figure 27 William Grant was the first Captain of the 2nd Brantford, Highland, Rifle Company. He served his country at the Sarnia frontier in 1864/65 and when the 38th Brant Battalion of Infantry was formed he became its first Paymaster.

Figure 28 J. J. Inglis was the first Lieutenant of the 2nd Brantford, Highland, Rifle Company eventually becoming its Captain.

The men apparently did go ahead ordering the cloth as Lt. Col. Wilkes on June 17th wrote to the Adjutant General advising that the cloth had arrived but that the men would not proceed any further without knowing that the company was gazetted. He stated that they had kept up their regular drill training during the winter and were well advanced in these exercises. He said that the company had scheduled a meeting on June 23rd to decide what to do. Some of the men were discouraged because of the wait. He requested an answer quickly advising that Mr. Grant would pay for a telegram. In the corner of the letter someone wrote: "*Yes in Class B, Ans. by telegraph, June 21, 62*". [158]

On June 21, 1862 Lt. Col. Wilkes again wrote to the Adjutant General and sent the following 2nd Service Roll: [159]

"*2nd Service roll of the #2 Brantford, Highland Rifle Company*
June 1862

We the undersigned agree to enrol ourselves as members of a Highland rifle corps of the county of Brant in Class B of the militia law of the province."

Austin, Alex	Hardie, Thomas	McKenzie, Alexander
Blacke, Edward	Hardy, Wm.	McLenon, James
Blythe, Thomas	Henry, Charles	McNaughton, James
Boyd, Robert	Henry, John	Nichol, James F.
Campbell, George	Johnston, B.	Nichol, Wm.
Campbell, Murdock	Kennedy, Wm.	Nicholson, Archibald
Carlyle, John	Laird, George	O'Brien, Wm.
Carlyle, Thomas	Laughton, John	Park, Robert
Collie, Wm.	Maclean, Wm.	Roddick, John B.
Cron, Archibald	Marshall, George	Russell, Robert
Fair, George	Mason, John	Rutherford, James
Fear, Samuel	McAulay, John	Singer, William
Fraser, David	McAulay, Phillip	Spencer, James
Fraser, Wm.	McEwen, D.	Tainsh, John
Gallie, David	McFarlain, Robert	Turner, James
Gardiner, John	McFarlane, John	Turner, Robert
Gibson, Alex	McFee, John	Walker, Charles
Gibson, Walter	McGiven, Daniel	Watson, L. B
Gill, George	McHaffie, John	Watt, Robert
Grant, Robert	McIntosh, Geo.	Webster, Alex
Greenlaw, Robert	McIntyre, Angus	Wilson, Alexander
Grierson, George	McIntyre, Peter	Wilson, Angus
Grierson, James	McIntyre, R.	Wilson, Stephen
Hardie, John	McKay, James	

On September 16th 1862 the company was inspected by Lt. Col. MacDougall and he complimented them. On parade were 1 Captain, 1 Lieutenant and 42 Non-commissioned officers and men. Their Highland uniform consisted of rifle green jackets, tartan trousers called trews with glengarries as head dress.

Forty-three of the company were uniformed and the materials for the clothing of the others was with the tailor.

MacDougall stated that the company made a very good appearance *"being young stout men and nearly all mechanics"*.

A room about 50 feet by 27 feet was secured for an armoury. By this time the company had nearly one hundred names on their roll. About sixty attended regularly.

Because of the excellent inspection the company was recommended to receive sixty rifles with accoutrements and an equal number of great coats. Four of the rifles were to be short Enfields with sword bayonet for the sergeants of the company. [160]

On November 25th 1863 Captain Grant wrote to the Adjutant General inquiring whether the government would be willing to match a $1000 donation from the Town of Brantford for the purpose of establishing a drill shed. Apparently there was a large building that could be purchased for about that amount.

Figure 29 The old Buck Stove works building was used in the early 1860s by Brantford's rifle companies for drill purposes.

Captain Grant seemed to be thinking of the future because he stated that the building would be large enough to accommodate a battalion. [161]

His letter was answered on December 4th and was not altogether satisfactory because he wrote back on December 10th expressing his displeasure. [162]

He stated that he had received a cheque for $330 which was the money for the company's annual drilling but "*I am at a loss to know what to do with those members of my corps who receive only $6.00 for what cost them over $12.00*". He also said that he would have a hard time explaining to his men that the uniforms are the property of the crown when they themselves had paid for them. He stated further that the government had not sent any compensation for care and storage of arms and that surely the government wasn't suggesting that the Captain bear the cost out of his own pocket.

On January 23, 1864 the Captain swore in his men which was required by the Volunteer Act. As a result of doing this he had to strike off the roll about twenty men. Just after that the company competed for a prize by being inspected. He was unfortunately unable to muster the required fifty men so the company could not compete. Captain Grant was very unhappy about this and complained that the other competing companies should have been required to first swear in their men. [163]

On July 14, 1864 Ensign M. X. Carr submitted his letter of resignation due to his acceptance of the job of Post Master of Paris Station. Sergeant David Spence was nominated and received the position of Ensign as his replacement.[164]

On December 11, 1864 Captain Grant wrote to the Brigade Major informing him that "*considerable excitement exists here with reference to a secret organization said to have an existence in our midst*". [165] This was the time of growing concern about the Fenians and, although never mentioned, it was probably this group to whom Captain Grant referred. He further stated "*yesterday morning I received a note from a friend residing in Buffalo urging me in the strongest terms to prepare for trouble*".

The biggest concern was the lack of security of the armoury where arms and ammunition were stored. The Captain was reluctant to make any bold moves because it would further excite the townspeople who were already concerned. He said if the major issued written orders then a guard would be placed over the arms. But he was unsure of any action and was seeking advice from a senior officer. "*If there is any foundation for the wild alarm I think the best way would be to place a guard of four or six men each night in the armouries*". He suggested that this could be done quickly and that they could be even safer by using certain signals previously agreed upon amongst themselves.

Figure 30 David Spence began as Ensign in the 2nd Brantford Rifles in 1864 and was appointed Commanding Officer of the 38th Battalion, Dufferin Rifles of Canada, in 1894.

David Spence was an officer in Capt. Grant's Highland Rifle Company. He was commissioned as Ensign in December 1864[166] from the rank of Sergeant. He was the first man from Brant County to obtain a 2nd Class certificate from the School of Military Instruction in 1864.[167] He eventually obtained a 1st Class certificate[168] and became the 38th's Adjutant and Drill Instructor.[169]

In private life he owned a mill on the canal bank in Brantford and a flour and feed store on Colborne Street.[170] He had the honour of commanding the 38th Battalion, Dufferin Rifles of Canada, in 1894.

The Hon. Dr. Bown had called on him with reference to the excitement prevailing in the town and said he had written a very strong letter to John A. Macdonald urging action by the government. The mayor planned to send a communication regarding the problem the next day.

"*Many little circumstances of a suspicious character are hourly detailed*" to Capt. Grant. "*Quite a number of gentlemen are inquiring if the government will supply them with arms and also if I will drill them.*"[171]

The Brigade Major in a communication marked, 'Private', stated, "*I am really very much alarmed about the safe keeping of some of the companies' arms*". He directed Capt. Grant to do nothing in a hurry to cause alarm and to gain as much information as possible. He suggested a guard could be put on the armoury but everything be kept quiet. He also was seeking some advice on what action should be taken from the Adjutant General's office.

Capt. Grant and his company didn't have long to attend to these issues because in a short time they would be sent off to the frontier as part of Canada's response to the St. Albans Raid.

The St. Albans Raid

On October 19, 1864 a band of about thirty Confederate soldiers, who had been staying secretly in Canada, slipped quietly across the U.S.-Canada border and, in the name of the Confederacy, raided the small Vermont town of St. Albans.

The following facts were reported in the local papers of the time. They came by twos and threes on different trains. About 3 p.m. parties of five each entered the three banks and demanded money threatening to shoot those who resisted. At the same time other raiders went to hotels and stables seizing the horses. The raid in all took less than one hour.[172]

While stealing the horses they met with some resistance and it is reported that two citizens were shot. As soon as horses were collected they headed north to return to Canada. North of St. Albans a third citizen was reported shot. Five of the raiders were eventually caught and tried by Canadian authorities. The Americans were so angry at the incident that they promptly cancelled the Reciprocity Treaty and for the first time in history imposed passports on persons entering the U.S. from Canada. They also requested extradition of the five prisoners to the U.S. [173]

The Canadian judge after a lengthy trial decided that the St. Albans raiders did not come within the provisions of the Extradition Treaty and he therefore discharged them. The judge's decision was that the raid was "a political crime". U.S. and many Canadians were outraged. [174]

The five raiders were again promptly rearrested, sent to Toronto and tried on charges of unlawfully conducting war against the U.S. resulting in four being discharged and the fifth granted bail. The Sarnia Observer reported *"that through the quibbles of Counsel and the blundering conclusions of so-called judges they have escaped punishment".* [175]

It was because of the offence and the outcome of the proceedings that Canadian troops were ordered to the border to guard against further infractions of Canada's status as a neutral country in relation to the American conflict. It was decided that #2 Brantford Rifles would be sent to Sarnia and Capt. Grant responded to the mobilization with the following telegram.

"Brantford Dec. 22, 1864

65 men sworn in and waiting orders. Send 15 rifle uniforms, 5 great coats, 5 rifles and belts. We have no knapsacks. Say when likely to be ordered out so that private arrangements can be made.

Wm. Grant
Highland Rifles"

Capt. Grant then telegraphed headquarters on December 23, 1864 saying private business interests required his presence until January 15th and asked if it would be possible for his Lieutenant to take the company to Sarnia where he would join them later. Three days later he received the following telegram.

"December 26, 1864
Capt. Grant

You will direct Lieut. Inglis to leave on Wed. morning next with your company with cooked rations for one day and proceed by train to Sarnia via Paris under command of Capt. Davis. A hot meal will be forwarded for the Company at London. You will ascertain before starting from Brantford the hour at which Capt. Davis with his company will arrive at the station and be prepared to join him there".

The citizens of Brantford were very supportive of the Highland Rifle Company. On December 23rd the Brant County Council wishing to express its support

"resolved that this Council express its high approval of the promptness with which the several companies of Volunteers have responded to the Call of the government for their services in preserving the strict neutrality of this province thereby showing their loyalty and willingness to uphold the government in its efforts to prevent this province from becoming involved in difficulties with the neighbouring States". [176]

Also in a public meeting it was decided to give the sum of $650, ten dollars for each man, to the Volunteers.

Some men from other companies who sought the honour and adventure of doing frontier duty wanted to join Capt. Grant's company. On December 24, 1864 Ensign Hiram Dickie of No. 1 Brantford Company wrote to headquarters requesting permission for a few of his men to do so. Ensign Dickie noted that Major Alger, Number 1 Company Captain, objected to the move.

On Tuesday at eight o'clock the same day as the vote to give the volunteers money, the company was marched to the Kerby Hall then put into two lines on either side of the Hall. [177]

Mayor James Weynes addressed the Captain and his men and presented them with the $650. The Captain gratefully accepted the money on behalf of his men. He said it was very opportune and acceptable to a great number of the company who depended solely on the work of their hands for their daily food and who without it could not purchase kit in the quantity required. Capt. Grant was followed by several other speakers. The company after giving three cheers returned to their armoury to prepare for their departure the following morning.

On Wednesday, the day the company departed, Capt. Grant telegraphed headquarters:

"December 28, 1864

No supplies except knapsacks received. Very great inconvenience. In consequence will send them on to Sarnia as they arrive here. Company left today. Will join company by fifteenth 15th Jany.
Wm. Grant"

Wednesday at 11 o'clock they proceeded to the railway station under escort of No. 1 Rifles. While there, awaiting the arrival of the York Rifles of Haldimand, they were briefly addressed by dignitaries of the Town. Three cheers were given for Queen Victoria, three for #1 Rifle Company and three for the mayor.[178]

The York Rifles arrived late around 12:30 p.m. and the two companies then proceeded to Sarnia. The force consisting of both companies numbered in all 131 men besides officers.

Upon arrival in Sarnia the troops were billeted in Halls Hotel. This barrack proved to be too small for two companies but it was endured for the entire tour of duty. [179] The officers were quartered in the private home of a patriotic individual who had vacated leaving it for their use. It was located close to the Wesleyan church. During the tour extra quarters were negotiated for and the replacement troops would be billeted in Halls Hotel and the Sarnia Agricultural Hall which had been specially equipped.

We are very fortunate that an account of the company's daily activities in Sarnia was preserved by a reporter as follows: [180]

"Daily Routine of the Volunteers

A correspondent of the London Free Press thus describes the daily routine of the Brantford and York Volunteers at present stationed in our town.

Reveille sounds at 6:30 a.m., breakfast at 7:30, morning drill at 9:00 for 30 minutes under the adjutant, commanding officer's parade at 10:30 for one hour and a half, dinner at 1 o'clock p.m.; afternoon parade and route march at 2 o'clock, at 6 o'clock tea roll calls after which may be seen a number of gallant volunteers on the ice with a Canadian girl on one side and a Yankee girl on the other...The bugle calls tattoo at 9 o'clock and then Uncle Sam's daughters find that our Canada girls have the advantage, for the former have to cross the boundary line to go home alone, while the latter are joined by their 'darling boys' and no doubt poison their minds against their fair American cousins. At 9:15 o'clock last post sounds and at 9:30 douse the glim (lights). Thus closes the performance of a days duty in barracks, and each succeeding day is but a repetition. Sunday excepted, when the men parade at 10:30 o'clock and then march off to their respective places of worship."

The visit of Brantford's Zion church minister, the Rev. Wm. Cochrane, to Sarnia, was a very popular event and was described in both the Brantford and Sarnia papers. He stayed several days preaching and delivered a lecture to the Volunteers and townspeople on 'Hedley Vicars the Christian Soldier'. Letters exchanged between Rev. Cochrane and the Volunteers were published in the papers. The Reverend was invited to extend his stay but commitments prevented this.[181]

Entertainment during free time is said to have involved ice skating, which was very popular especially with the young ladies of Sarnia. Also one of the Sarnia libraries loaned books and local people left newspapers at the barracks. Rev. Cochrane began to solicit Brantford citizens to send reading materials to the men. The Brantford citizenry were also sending letters to the volunteers which eventually were published in the Brantford Expositor. [182]

Baseball was a popular sport played by the men and around mid March an accident occurred to Private Robert Kerr of the Highland Rifles. He was playing ball with some others, one of whom ran against him and accidentally knocked him down. He was injured and it was not believed he would live through the night. His parents in Brantford were notified by telegraph and his brother visited him in the morning. Fortunately Kerr did survive and returned home safely. [183]

Though no incursion of neutrality occurred while the company was at the frontier, there was an interesting incident involving the force. Headlines in the local paper read, *"The Brantford Volunteers Actively Engaged"* [184] It seems that a rebellion had started in the local jail by about 30 prisoners. One of the prisoners obtained a key and they escaped. The jailer ran to the warning bell to alert citizens but the prisoners had anticipated this, cut the rope and tied the jailer up with it.

The County Sheriff appealed for help to the Volunteer force about 10:00 p.m. Soldiers were then sent out in sections but none of the prisoners could be found. The next day the entire force made a large search pursuing the fugitives but none were captured.

The Globe reported in March that all thirty companies along the complete frontier would be replaced May 1, 1865 with 21 companies. This was to enable other companies to *'perfect themselves in drill and military duties'.* [185]

It was decided that the Brantford and York Volunteer companies would be replaced on Friday April 28, 1865 by the London and Ottawa volunteer companies.

Farewell and welcoming ceremonies were a final highlight to a very successful tour of duty. On the Friday before leaving, officers of the two companies were invited to a farewell dinner. On the Tuesday prior to leaving a picnic was given for all men of the companies. The commanding officers decided to order a troop review and general field day before the picnic. [186]

On the common, north of town, at 2:00 p.m. the force assembled and went through various drill movements ending in a mock battle. This was watched by a large gathering of Sarnia citizens. Afterwards the picnic was held.

On Friday morning, despite the cold and drizzling rain there was a general turnout of the citizens for the departure. The company had been ordered by headquarters to leave on the 8:30 a.m. train and were due in Paris at 2:00 p.m. From there they would take the Buffalo-Goderich train to the Brantford station. On the train ride home they were met at the stations by crowds of spectators who had gathered to salute them. At Watford they met the London company which was travelling to replace them.

The rain they had encountered in Sarnia had become worse when they reached Brantford. A large reception at the railroad depot had been planned but was not possible due to the inclement weather.

In the evening, Captain Grant, his officers and men were given an official welcome home at a supper at the Brant Hotel. The large dining hall was filled by an enthusiastic group of citizens. The usual patriotic toasts were given and duly responded to. Speeches were made by several prominent citizens ending in a speech by Capt. Grant. He noted that the company had improved greatly in their drill and discipline, had gained a good name amongst the Sarnia citizens and had won the distinction of being pronounced by the Inspecting Officers, second to no company on frontier service.[187]

There was also some very good singing by local citizens. The following song, arranged by Colour Sergeant McHaffie, was sung by the whole company in full chorus. [188]

"The Highlanders I hear them say,
Hurrah! Hurrah!
Will be marched home the first of May,
Hurrah! Hurrah!
Then let our Brantford friends look out,
And welcome with a joyful about.
And we'll all feel gay,
When we go marching home.

No battles fought, no victories won,
Hurrah! Hurrah!
The raiders told our guns did shun,
Hurrah! Hurrah!
No golden medal or wooden leg,
To decorate a Highland lad,
So we'll all feel gay,
When we go marching home.

Our wives will meet us when we land,
Hurrah! Hurrah!
To welcome home the gallant band,
Hurrah! Hurrah!
Who left their homes to volunteer
To guard the Western frontier
And we'll all feel gay,
When we go marching home.

Our sweethearts too, will all be there,
Hurrah! Hurrah!
With joyful abouts they'll rend the air
Hurrah! Hurrah!
We'll kiss them all and so will they,
And both wish for the happy day
And we'll all feel gay,
When we go marching home.

With sixty five we marched away
Hurrah! Hurrah!
And sixty five we count today
Hurrah! Hurrah!
So wives and mothers be of good cheer,
For nothing now you have to fear;
But we'll all feel gay,
When we go marching home.

To all you men that staid at home
Hurrah! Hurrah!
A word I'd speak, and I am done,
Hurrah! Hurrah!
When your country makes a call,
Be ready in the ranks to fall;
And we'll all feel gay,
When we go marching home."

Members of #2 Brantford Highland Rifle Company who served at the Sarnia Frontier 1864-65[189]

Ashton, J.
Black, J.
Blacker, R.
Blythe, T.
Bulmer, W.
Clark, A.
Coyle, W.
Crooks, A.
Danskin, J.
Ditchfield, S.
Dougherty, J.
Fergusson, A.
Fergusson, J.
Foulds, J.
Frazer, W.
Gibson, A.
Gidden, W.
Good, J.
Goodson, A. A
Gordon, T.
Grant, Captain W.
Grantham, G.
Hammond, J. H.
Howarth, W.
Hunter, Cpl 1st N.
Inglis, Lieut. J. J.
Jamieson, R.
Jones, C. A.
Kerr, R.
Mart, W.
McCauley, Cpl 3rd P.
McHaffie, Colour Sgt. J.
McIntosh, P.
Montgomery, J.
Nesbit, J.
Nicol, Cpl 2nd Wm.
Nicoll, J. F.
Nicoll, W.
O'Neill, J. F.
Palmer, W.
Patterson, J. W.
Pillsworth, J.
Poole, Sergeant H.
Reed, E. H.
Reed, H. W.
Reed, J.
Reed, M.
Reed, S.
Renwick, T.
Robson, H.
Rowe, J.
Russell, Sergeant R.
Rutherford, D.
Rutherford, J.
Scott, T. O
Spence, Ensign D.
Spencer, Lance-Cpl 2nd J.
Stewart, A.
Vaughan, J.
Wade, B. J.
Walker, C.
Walker, J. H.
Wallace, R.
Wilson, F. D.
Wilson, H.
Wilson, Lance-Cpl 1st R.
Wright, J. G.

For an example of what type of men joined a volunteer company several of the 2nd Brantford men are listed with occupations:

Capt. William Grant	clothier
Sgt. Robert Russell	Richie & Russell
Bugler John O'Neil	conductor
Cpl. Robert Willson	law student (Cameron & Willson)
Private Charles Heyd	clerk
Private Thomas Gordon	labourer
Private Robert Watt	carpenter
Private James Wright	engine driver

Highland Company Band

In mid 1866 the first article on the Highland Company Band appeared in the local newspapers.[190] Band concerts were regularly being held at the Kerby Hall, the Town Hall or Alexandra Park. Both Number 1 and the Highland Band were popular entertainment at various events such as local picnics or military reviews.[191]

Annual Supper

Like all militia companies the Highland Rifles had an Annual Supper for company members. Being a Highland company the men were very proud of their Scottish roots. The supper was held on the birthday of Scottish poet Robbie Burns whom they called 'the most gigantic spirit that trod the earth'. The usual toasts were made, elegant recitations given and songs sung. [192]

Several pay lists are contained in the addendum on page 104 and an officers list on page 110.

Brantford Volunteer Review of 1863 [193]

On September 3rd , 1863 a military review of about 2,200 volunteer militiamen occurred at Brantford. Newspapers reported there were from 15,000 to 20,000 spectators. The Review was held on the old exhibition ground which was just a short march from the train station. The exhibition building had been enlarged by the addition of two wings and stands had been erected which sat 2,600 spectators.

The weather was excellent with a clear sky and cool breeze. Visitors began arriving at 7 a.m. and by ten the streets were crowded. The two railway companies had agreed to transport the militia at reduced prices and at 9 a.m. the first train arrived. The companies of militia were smartly marched over to a large railway building for refreshments then on to the review ground. Staff officers then conducted them to their positions on the field. The companies continuously arrived from 9 a.m. to 1 p.m. while the Burford Cavalry provided crowd control.

The volunteers were positioned on the left with the Artillery on the right and the Royal Artillery and the Rifle Brigade on the extreme right. The whole line is said to have been about one mile across. In total there were 41 rifle or infantry companies, the Goderich Foot Artillery, the Hamilton Field Battery and the St. Thomas and London Cavalry. The furthest company was the Windsor militia coming a distance of 164 miles.

At 1 p.m. Major-General Napier and several other staff officers inspected the men then stood while the three battalions marched past in slow and quick march.

"They then formed en mass, wheeled into contiguous columns, threw out skirmishers for the purpose of engaging or uncovering a supposed enemy; the skirmishers having been driven in, the first Brigade advanced, deployed into line, and after firing a volley or two, they formed squares and the Cavalry charged. The enemy proving too strong for them, they retired through the second Brigade, which moved up, supported by Artillery on the flanks. The enemy having brought up a heavy force of Cavalry, squares were again formed to resist them; ...a company of Cavalry here charged past the squares. The infantry again deployed into line (deployments were made from the right, left and centre, to thoroughly test them) and advanced and opened a galling fire on the foe, supported by Artillery on the right. We might state that the precision was beautiful with which the Rifle Brigade returned by fours from right of companies and closed on right company. The Review finished up by the troops forming into close columns by Battalions, advancing in slow time, halting and giving a general salute."

The reviewing officer, General Napier, addressed the parade and complimented them on these movements. He then dismissed them and they marched company by company to the exhibition building where a sumptuous meal had been prepared for all 2,200 men.

In 1863 Brantford was leading the way in preparing the province's volunteers to act together as a brigade.

3rd Brantford Infantry Company

The 3rd Brantford Infantry Company was gazetted on June 1, 1866.[194] There is little history for this company within the ten year period covered by this book. In the local newspaper it was described as: [195]

"Brantford Infantry Company

In the Official Gazette of Saturday last, the Brantford Infantry company is gazetted under the following officers. Henry Lemmon, Captain, John Ballachey, Lieutenant, and John Minore, Ensign. There has been no delay on the part of the Government in recognizing this company, as the application with the names attached was only before the proper authorities some six days previous to being gazetted. The arms, accoutrements and clothing will be here with the least possible delay. We are perfectly satisfied that this company will present in appearance second to none in the country, as they are a splendid body of men, fit companions in arms to the unrivalled rifles we have in town."

Figure 31 Henry Lemmon was the first Captain of the 3rd Brantford Infantry Company.

Henry Lemmon was a very public spirited yet controversial figure in Brantford. At various times he served on the school board, as a justice of the peace, on the committee to create Brant's monument and twice on the Dominion Census Committee. He lived on Nelson Street in 1875. He was a Worshipful County Master of the #360 Orange Lodge and an accomplished musician and singer often entertaining at town festivities. In his professional life he was editor and publisher of the Brantford Courier newspaper. Through his paper he was very outspoken in his views which often created friction. He was extreme in his likes and dislikes and often had to defend himself from verbal assaults. He was also a staunch supporter of the militia. He served in the 1st Brant Battalion Sedentary militia becoming a Lieutenant in 1856. During the exciting time of the Fenian Raid of 1866 he was authorized to raise and lead a company of volunteers. In his later years he was affectionately referred to as 'The Major'.

Figure 32 John Ballachey was the first Lieutenant of the 3rd Brantford Infantry Company and was appointed Commanding Officer of Brant's 38th Battalion , Dufferin Rifles of Canada, in 1887.

Captain Lemmon used his newspaper to recruit volunteers with the following advertisement:

" VOLUNTEERS WANTED

Those desirous of forming a new Volunteer company will please hand in their names at once, to either Mr. T. B McMahon or Mr. B.F. Fitch

Brantford, June 9th, 1866"

He also communicated with those who were presently in the company. The following is an example:

"ATTENTION

Brantford Infantry Company

The Brantford Infantry Company will meet for Drill at No. 1 Rifle Company armoury on Tuesday evening next, the 12th inst. at 7 o'clock sharp.

Henry Lemmon, Captain *Brantford, June 8th, 1866"*[196]

The #3 Brantford Company was gazetted in very little time. The Service Roll dated May 22, 1866 was sent by Capt. Lemmon and was then sent on to the Adjutant General's office on May 25th by the Brigade Major.

The Hon. John A. Macdonald also sent a letter dated May 25th to the Adjutant General recommending Capt. Lemmon's company in very favourable words. One week later the company was gazetted.[197]

"Service Roll of the 3rd Brant Infantry Company of volunteer militia under the command of Captain Henry Lemmon. May 1866

We, whose names are hereunto subscribed, declare that we, have taken the oath of allegiance to our Sovereign and voluntarily agree to serve in the Brant Infantry company of volunteer militia under the conditions of service for the government of the Volunteer Militia Force of Canada, as set forth in the existing militia laws of the province."

Ballachey, Lieut. John
Ballachey, George Jr.
Ballintine, Wm.
Barton, Henry
Beattie, Richard
Bowes, J.
Boyd, Joseph
Brooke, Robert
Brooks, John
Brown, John
Bungy, A.
Campbell, Arch.
Carson, W.
Clark, John A.
Clench, Ralfe
Dill, Thos.
Doherty, Hugh
Draper, Charles
Fallis, John
Fallis, James
Ferguson, Andrew
Finlayson, H.
Foster, Charles
Gardner, Henry
Glover, Thomas
Glover, Robert
Gray, William
Gray, James
Hunt, Charles
Johnstone, ---
Kay, John
Kenny, Thomas
Lemmon, Capt. Henry
Masterson, John
McCann, John
McLean, S.
McLean, Robt.
McLean, Joseph
Minore, Ensign John
Muma, Jacob W.
Parkin, William
Perry, James E.
Rowe, P.
Shaw, Alex K.
Smyth, Isaac
Stewart, ---
Strong, Thos.
Sutton, N. L.
Vancleve, Alonzo
Walsh, Wm.
Wells, William
Welsh, James
Whiffin, Jarvis
Wilson, Christopher
Wye, John H.

The letter from the Hon. John A. Macdonald recommending Number 3 company read as follows:

"Dept. Of Attorney General, U. C.
Ottawa May 25, 1866
Private

My dear Colonel

I send you a private note from Mr. Henry Lemmon Editor & proprietor of the 'Brantford Courier' and as you see an enthusiastic friend of mine. He is a very respectable man and conducts a very loyal and respectable Journal and I would like to oblige him if it can be done. Will you be kind enough to return his letter.

Yours faithfully
John A. Macdonald

Col. MacDougall
Adjutant General of Militia
Ottawa"

In November the Brantford Town Council passed a motion which granted the company $17.50 to pay for six months rent of an armoury. [198]

An example of the occupations of the men can be seen from the following:

Capt. Henry Lemmon	proprietor & publisher Brantford Courier
Ensign John Minore	confectioner
James Gray	manufacturer of agricultural implements
Henry Gardner	saddler at Gill & Gardner
Christopher Wilson	boot and shoe maker
John H. Wye	medical doctor
Alex Shaw	machinist
Thomas Kenny	proprietor of Dominion Hotel
James Welsh	tinsmith
John Brooks	boiler maker

A list of officers is contained in the addendum on page 110.

Mount Pleasant Infantry Company

The Mount Pleasant Infantry Company was officially gazetted on January 30, 1863.[199] According to Major W. N. Alger it was one of the companies that received its initial encouragement to organize from himself and Dr. Bown MPP for East Brant when they toured the county in 1862 holding meetings on Volunteer Militia. [200]

The first Captain of the Mount Pleasant Company was Allan Wallace Ellis. The first Lieutenant was William E. Phelps and the first Ensign Robert Eadie.

Allan Wallace Ellis was a farmer in Mount Pleasant by occupation. His grandfather was a United Empire Loyalist and was among the first settlers of Mt. Pleasant. R. C. Muir in his military history speaks very highly of the Ellis family's long-standing and honourable military history. Ellis had served in the cavalry raised during the Mackenzie rebellion of 1837. In 1857 he was commissioned as Ensign in the 3rd Brant Battalion sedentary militia.

Figure 33 Allan Wallace Ellis was the first Captain of the Mount Pleasant Infantry Company.

The first Service Roll of the Mount Pleasant Company contained the following names. [201]

"<u>Service roll of the Mt. Pleasant Infantry Company</u>
January 1863

We the undersigned hereby enrol ourselves as members of an infantry company in the 3rd Battalion of Brant in accordance with the militia law of the province."

Armstrong, James	Gallic, David	Owen, Walter M.
Biggar, William	Grace, James	Phelps, ---
Boyd, Robt.	Guest, Richard	Phelps, S.
Bryce, George	Hardy, David	Phelps, Wm. E.
Bryce, John	Hartley, Robert	Raw, John
Campbell, Alexander	Heaton, Crosley	Robertson, Curry
Campbell, Murdock	Malcolm, Finlay	Rutherford, David
Chatterson, Soloman	Marquis, Duncan	Rutherford, Donald
Clark, James	McEwen, Archibald	Rutherford, James
Cook, W.	McEwen, Peter	Ryan, William
Eadie, James	McEwen, Wm. Geo.	Smith, Frances Allen
Eadie, Robt.	McFarlane, John	Smith, Walter
Ellis, Allan W.	McLennan, Robert	Thomas, David H.
Fairchild, Christopher	McPherson, Angus	Tomlinson, William
Fitzpatrick, Edward	Murray, Walter	Wedgerfield, William
Franklin, William		

The second Lieutenant and second Captain of the company was <u>Crosley Heaton</u> who came to Brant County at the age of 16 with his brother Jonas settling in Mt. Pleasant. He bought a farm of 80 acres and resided there for 30 years. He then sold the farm and conducted a general business for 7 years. In 1879 he moved to Brantford and became a dealer in boots and shoes on Colborne Street. He was a reformer in politics and a member of the Methodist church. [202]

Captain Ellis wrote of the early months of the company in a letter to the Adjutant General of Militia in the following words: [203]

"For the first six months our places for drill were barns, blacksmiths etc. Nothing daunted however, we persisted. In May we received our arms. Delighted with the prospect then before us we at once rented a room for an armoury and made the necessary fixtures which was highly approved of by the Brigade Major. Yet not being satisfied with this we set about building a drill shed and it is now completed which the Brigade Major says is second to none in his military district. Size 40 by 70. Inside of this we have built an armoury taking off 6 feet from half the width of the building which leaves us plenty of room still."

Figure 34 Mount Pleasant Drill Shed (centre) was built in 1863 on the north-west corner lot of Mt. Pleasant Street and County Road 26.

In order to pay for the debt still remaining on the volunteer drill shed the men raised money through events such as the Military Concert held on October 23, 1863. Several vocalists from Brantford, the Simcoe Amateur Minstrel Troupe with Professor Klophet on piano were engaged to perform. Tickets were 25 cents. [204]

In October 1863 Capt. Ellis decided to resign his Captaincy. He noted, "*reluctantly - owing to circumstances over which I have no control I am compelled to tender my resignation.*"[205]

The Brigade Major in recommending the resignation said Capt. Ellis and Lieut. Heaton simply could not agree. In April 1864 Capt. Ellis recommended Thomas Racey as the new commanding officer. In July Racey wrote to the Brigade Major asking to be gazetted Captain as he had been duly elected.[206] For reasons we do not know Mr. Racey did not become Captain of the Mount Pleasant Company.[207] Lieut. Heaton led the company in that rank until May 25, 1866. His promotion to Captain came about three weeks into the mobilization against the Fenians.

As mentioned in more detail in Chapter 2, the company served honourably in Mt. Pleasant and Paris during the Fenian crisis.

After becoming part of the 38th Brant Battalion of Infantry the company existed for another 3 ½ years. In official militia records it is stated that the company had failed in its reorganization. R. C Muir states in his book on Brant militia that, "*After the resignation of their first officers this company gradually became inefficient and was removed from the list of Volunteer militia*". [208] The company officially ceased to exist on February 6, 1869.[209]

The following are some of the civilian occupations of the Mount Pleasant militia men:

Crosley Heaton	farmer, merchant
William Vivian	millwright
Samuel Fear	wagon maker
Archibald McEwen	farmer, J. P
Richard Guest	butcher
William Ryan	labourer
Walter Murray	farmer
George Bryce	blacksmith
Peter McEwen	farmer

Figure 35 William Vivian of Oakland Township was a Corporal in the Mt. Pleasant Company and a Fenian raid veteran serving at Paris in June 1866.

The pay lists from 1864 to 1866 are contained in the Addendum on page 105 and an officers list on page 110.

Burford Militia

In 1866 there were two militia units gazetted in the Burford area. The Burford Infantry Company was gazetted on August 17, 1866[210] and the Burford Cavalry Troop on September 7, 1866.[211]

Burford and Oakland townships are the areas in Brant County that do have a comprehensive record of military history for the period in question thanks to Major R. C Muir of Burford. Major Muir was a contemporary of that time and also a military enthusiast. His book, The Early Political and Military History of Burford, reports on the military happenings and is recommended as a source for Burford militia history. A short article that Muir wrote in 1927, and not seen published in some time, describes the beginnings of the volunteer units and is reprinted in full. [212]

Figure 36 The first meeting of the Burford Volunteer Infantry Company was held in Hearns Hall, which was the upper floor of Brock Miller's store formerly attached to Roetin Products, 106 King Street, Burford.

"BURFORD WAS ONCE CENTRE OF ACTIVITY OF VOLUNTEERS
by R. C Muir

Immediately after the invasion of the fighting members of the Fenian Brotherhood, at Fort Erie, in the early morning of June 1, 1866, the Government of the two Canadas awoke to the fact that the Canadian volunteer could be depended upon to defend the country and repel the invader in any similar emergency and they immediately took steps to largely augment the force by the addition of new troops of cavalry, batteries of artillery and companies of infantry and rifles. Edmund Yeigh, formerly an ensign in Colonel Chas. S. Perley's 5th Brant Militia, suggested the formation of an infantry company in Burford, and a meeting was held in 'Hearn's Hall,' now the upper part of Mr. Brock Miller's emporium of trade, records R. C Muir in the Burford Advance. A committee was formed and Mr. Yeigh was authorized to communicate with the Hon. John A. Macdonald, then minister of militia in the Cartier-Macdonald Government and secure his consent to organize a unit of the active militia, to be known as 'The Burford Infantry Company.'

The necessary permission having been granted from Ottawa, where the Government had permanently settled previous to Confederation, the following names were submitted to the Department for approval: For Captain, Ira Wooden; Lieutenant, Claudius Byrne; Ensign, Edmund Yeigh. The Official Gazette of August 17, 1866, contained their temporary appointments, pending their attendance at a military school and the possession of qualified certificates. Ira Wooden failed to comply with the conditions and after three months was retired, and Ensign Yeigh, with the consent of Lieut. Byrne, was promoted captain, November 6, 1866

During the winter of 1868 Sergts. Stephen Wetmore and Gilbert French had qualified for promotion, and when Captain Yeigh resigned on July 16, 1869, Lieut. Byrne became a captain, Stephen Wetmore lieutenant, and Gilbert French ensign. These officers held their positions until May 28, 1875, when Captain Byrne was retired, Stephen Wetmore promoted to the command of the company and Sergt. Rory Johnston lieutenant. At this period an economical Government reduced the strength of troops of cavalry and companies of infantry and rifles and allowed two officers to each unit.

Gilbert French had taken part in the famous Red River Expedition, under Sir Garnet Wolseley for the suppression of the Riel Rebellion, and like most soldiers who have seen active service, on his return he found the home guard too tame for his military energies. Gilbert French and Rory Johnston, clothed in the scarlet uniform of Burford's first volunteer infantry company, were, in their day, fine specimens of the Canadian volunteer, and were both popular with their men and their superior officers.

It has been said that infantry soldiers outlive those of any other branch of the service. Of the charter members of this old company, we have still with us Lieut. Rory Johnston, Sergt. John Charles and the still youthful Bradley Van Horn. There are also Sergts. Angus Johnston and Joseph Hunter, who joined in 1868 and were connected with the company as long as it existed in Burford and after that with the Burford Dragoons.

WAS INSTRUCTOR

Immediately after the enrolment of the recruits, none of the officers being capable of imparting instruction in drill and discipline, Mr. Aaron B. McWilliams, a past candidate from the Toronto Military School, was appointed by the Government as instructor, when not only privates but officers as well, received their first lessons in military movements. Daily evening parades were held, first in the school grounds, and, when the weather grew cooler, in the Kerby Hotel barn, located opposite to where is now the new Burford Advance building.

During the sixties and for many years thereafter the country's administrators did not exercise that growing paternalism , so much in evidence during later years, made possible by the extravagant outlay of hundreds of millions of borrowed cash. The first minister of militia of the new Dominion Government made no provision for suitable buildings for the care and storage of arms and equipment or for the exercising of the volunteers belonging to independent units, refusing to borrow money for the purpose. It was demonstrated that all the country could afford to do without running into debt was to assist those communities who were willing to help themselves by providing most of the necessary funds for the erection of such buildings. The luxurious and commodious armories which now dot the country were beyond the most sanguine dreams of the first Canadian volunteers. The latter were, however, well armed, clothed and equipped and with frequent practice became to a man excellent marksmen.

MOVED FOR DRILL SHED

The officers of the company now commenced a movement for the construction of a drill shed, according to the regulations then in force. Government aid was to be granted to the extent of $250 for all one company drill sheds, the balance of the cost to made up by:

1st - Grant by county council
2nd - Grant by township council
3rd - Contributions from other sources.

In the first place, a suitable site had to be provided and deeded over to Her Majesty's Government.

All drill sheds, towards the construction of which Government aid was given, had to become exclusively Government property, as well as the ground on which they were built, of which latter a proper title must be made to Her Majesty's Government and before such aid was given.

All drill sheds were constructed on one Government plan, provided by the militia department. The militia department did not undertake to let out the contracts for the erection of drill sheds, nor to superintend the work during the construction of the building, but the payment of the Government grants in aid was subject to such inspection when completed as the Government thought proper to prescribe.

In addition to this, it was necessary to furnish a certificate from the inspector, showing that he had inspected the building and found it had been erected and completed according to the plan supplied by the militia department , also a certificate from the county crown attorney to the effect that he had examined the title and found it and the conveyance sufficient to vest the legal title in the Crown.

DONATED LAND

It was while working under these adverse conditions that Captain Yeigh decided to donate a piece of ground of sufficient size, on the north-west corner of his estate on King Street east, and then with indefatigable energy started out to interview the county and township councils, and with their aid, and by means of entertainments and private subscriptions, raise the necessary funds, or secure sufficient guarantee that they could be raised before commencing operations. How Captain Yeigh and his friends succeeded may be gathered from the fact that by the fall of 1867 the 'Burford drill shed' was entirely completed and ready for inspection. The perseverance and assiduous efforts of these first officers of the Burford Infantry Company, like those of many other rural units, have long been forgotten, but should be remembered with interest by their successors, for it was by just such earnest, continuous work on the part of the officers of the first active volunteer militia and the hearty co-operation of the rank and file that the force for many years was kept alive.

DOCUMENTS FORWARDED

On the completion of the drill shed the following documents were forwarded to the militia department at Ottawa:

'Drill Shed at Burford, County of Brant.
I certify that a drill shed has been erected to the pattern plan supplied by the militia department, in Burford in the County of Brant, the size of which drill shed is 50 x 30. And the cost of erection of same, inclusive of the value of the land, amounts to the sum of $800, as per vouchers attached, the funds of the payment of which has been contributed as follows:

Grant by County Council	*$200*
Grant by Township Council	*200*
Received from other sources	*150*
Government Grant	*250*
Total	*$800*

The above named drill shed being completed and the title of the land on which it is erected having been made to Her Majesty, I now make application for the issue of a cheque in favour of Levi Jones for $250, the same being the amount of the government and as above stated.

(Signed) Edmund Yeigh, Captain
To the Militia Department, Ottawa Com. Burford Inf. Co.'

'Inspector's Certificate

I certify that I have inspected the above named drill shed and found that it has been erected and completed according to the pattern plan and the specifications therefor supplied by the militia department'. (No government inspector appeared).
'County Crown Attorney's Certificate

I certify that I have examined the title to the land being at Burford, in the County of Brant, upon which the above named drill shed has been erected and found it and the conveyance sufficient to vest the legal title of the same in the Crown.

(Signed) G. R. Van Norman
To the Militia Department, Ottawa County Crown Attorney
Brantford, September 10, 1867.'

The name of the contractor who erected the Burford drill shed was Levi G. Jones.

The new drill shed was formally opened by a grand military concert, talented vocalists from Brantford and the magnificent band of the 7th Royal Fusiliers, then stationed in the Kerby House Block, assisting in the entertainment.

BIRTHDAY CONCERTS

The Queen's Birthday concerts, held under the auspices of the officers of the company, were for many years an annual and important event in the life of the village. Many old-time exhibitions were also held in the commodious shed, such as the two-hour walking matches, the velocipede instruction school, whose agent, with his 5-foot front and 12-inch rear wheel required several assistants to hold his pupils in position. Most of the latter, found this mode of locomotion too complicated and dangerous for their daily use over the rough roads which existed at that period. Fifty years ago it was much more difficult to dispose of a single velocipede than half a dozen motor cars in this era.

On several occasions the South Brant nominations for political candidates and other public gatherings met in the drill shed and for some time it was used as a skating rink.

The Burford cavalry had taken no steps to ask aid from any source for the erection of a drill shed or armory, as their work was done entirely outside. During Capt. Bingham's tenure of command the arms and equipment were held in Bishopsgate, and when Lieut. Wm. Marshall assumed command a small but comfortable building on King Street west, the property of Sergt.-Major W. H. Serpell was secured and continued to be used until the year 1876, when the militia department, through the D. A. G. at Toronto, authorized the officers of the Burford cavalry to construct an armory in one end of the drill shed and also gave them permission to use the shed when necessary.

A suitable room was, by the exertions of the officers soon provided, the stores removed therein and Sergt. Daniel Dunn placed in charge.

The building now continued to be used conjointly by the Burford Cavalry and the Rifle Company up to the year 1883 when the headquarters of the latter were transferred to Brantford and the cavalry then became sole occupants. When the troop was reorganized as a squadron in 1898, additional and improved saddle racks were introduced and other improvements made in the armory to accommodate the increased strength. This was done at the entire expense of the officer commanding the squadron.

Economy and frugality in public expenditure was continued, and not only preached but practised by successive Federal Governments, particularly to any grants connected with the militia department.

On the completion and occupancy of the fine new armory on King Street west, the old drill shed was condemned and disposed of to the South Brant Agricultural Society. Owing to the nature of its construction, grave doubts were entertained as to the possibility of its holding together if moved to its new site 'en masse,' as many similar buildings had collapsed without being moved. As only the choicest timber had been used in its construction the excellent manner in which the work had been executed by Contractor Levi C. Jones, and the services of an expert and experienced mover, it was safely rolled across the fields to the fair ground, where it served as a commodious exhibition building until destroyed by fire some 15 years ago."

Burford Infantry Company

The Brantford Expositor reported in August 1866 [213]

"The Burford Rifles

Among the volunteer infantry companies recently gazetted, are the Burford Rifles. The officers have been duly appointed as follows - To be Captain, Ira C. Wooden; Lieutenant, Claudius Byrne; Ensign, Edmund Yeigh. The selection of officers has been judiciously made, and we confidently expect that the Burford Company will soon equal in efficiency any volunteer company in the Country."

On June 8th, Edmund Yeigh wrote to headquarters saying, "*As a Justice of the Peace...I have been appealed to by many young men desirous of being asked to help defend our country. - will you accept a company of vols?"* [214] This letter was written one week after the Fenian Raid. Headquarters replied that the government could not arm and equip any more companies at present. [215] On July 11th Yeigh again wrote saying that since a publication of the Attorney General's report about the Ridgeway battle he had been led to believe that his company might be authorized. He also added that the Brant Battalion being formed would desire another company. Therefore he repeated his offer of a company. We don't know of the answer to this correspondence but on July 19, a Service Roll for the Burford Infantry Company was sent to Brigade Major Villiers. [216]

Figure 37 Edmund Yeigh was the first Ensign and second Captain of the Burford Infantry Company.

Edmund Yeigh was the only son of Jacob Yeigh who was a veteran of the War of 1812 and the Mackenzie Rebellion of 1837. During the latter he sided with Mackenzie then fled to the U.S. Edmund inherited and managed his father's estate in Burford on Concession 7. In public life he served as a Justice of the Peace. He was also a strong force in 1866 helping organize the Burford Volunteer Infantry becoming its second Captain. R. C Muir describes Yeigh as a forceful speaker at the initial meeting of the company.

On August 9th Yeigh tried to get some political support and wrote to MPP David Christie asking him to exert his influence to get the company gazetted. He also advised that Captain Grant was very anxious that the company should be organized. [217]

Christie wrote to the Adjutant General's office on August 14th and lobbied for the Burford company. He states, "*I can speak confidently on behalf of the Burford company...I feel assured that they will discharge their duty to their Queen and Country."* [218] Three days later on August 17th the company was officially gazetted.

1st Service Roll of the Burford Infantry Company, July 1866[219]

"Service Roll of the Burford Infantry Company of Volunteer Militia under the command of Captain Ira C. Wooden. We, whose names are hereunto subscribed, declare that we have taken the Oath of Allegiance to the Sovereign and that we voluntarily agree to serve in the Burford Infantry Company of Volunteer Militia, under the conditions of service for the government of the volunteer militia force of Canada, as set forth in the existing militia laws of the Province."

Bouey, Alexander
Bouey, Angus
Bouey, Hector
Bouey, John
Briers, Henry
Briers, Peter
Briers, William
Brown, Charles W.
Brown, John H.
Byrne, Lieut. Claudius
Catton, Alfred
Caven, Robert
Charles, Frederick
Charles, John L.
Chisnoll, Hugh
Findlay, John
Forsyth, G. H.
Fowler, Alexander
Fowler, George
French, Gilbert
Hanmer, David G.
Henderson, Judson
Holder, James
Jackson, Joseph
Johnston, Rory
Jones, James R.
Jones, Thomas
McHanskill, Allan
McWilliams, James
McWilliams, Wm.
Monley, Henry
Padfield, G. A.
Shine, Timothy
Van Horn, Bradley
Wetherbee, Freemin
Wetmore, Stephen
Whale, George
Whale, John
Wooden, Capt. Ira C.
Yeigh, Ensign. Edmund

2nd Service Roll of the Burford Infantry Company, September 1866[220]

Berry, John
Bouey, Angus
Bouey, Hector
Bouey, John
Briers, Peter
Briers, William
Byrne, Lieut. Claudius
Catton, Alfred
Charles, Fred
Charles, John
Crysler, Edward
Crysler, Jesse
Elleby, Joseph
Farrel, Hiram
Farrel, Robert
Fox, Thomas
French, Gilbert
Griffin, Henry
Henderson, Judson
Holder, James
Johnston, John
Johnston, Rory
Lane, George
McCaskill, Allan
McCurdy, Charles
Munroe, John
Padfield, George
Padfield, John
Rush, Richard
Sharpe, James
Singer, Arbon
Tillison, Joshua
Tillison, Levi
Van Horn, Bradley
Wetmore, Sgt. Stephen
Whale, George
Whale, John
Whelpley, Cpl. Elijah
Wooden, Captain Ira
Yeigh, Ensign Edmund

Figure 38 Stephen Wetmore (right) was one of the first Sergeants of the Burford Infantry Company and was promoted to Captain in 1875. Rory Johnston (left) was one of the first members of the company and was promoted to Lieutenant in 1879.

In October the uniforms arrived in Paris from Ottawa, were brought to Burford and distributed. The soldiers received an issue of tunics, trousers, shakos (head dress) and great coats. The uniforms were supposedly of high quality made in England in the traditional infantry style. The tunics were scarlet, the trousers blue and they wore shakos as head-dress.[221]

The Burford Infantry Company continued as a unit of the 38th Brant Battalion until May 11, 1883 when it was removed from Burford to Brantford and gazetted a City Battalion company.[222] A list of officers is contained in the Addendum on page 110.

Burford Troop of Cavalry

Brantford Expositor reported in September, 1866:

"Burford Cavalry

The Burford troop of cavalry having been ordered to organize by the Minister of Militia, and having provided themselves with equipment in consequence, is placed on the list of the Volunteer Militia as a special case. To be Captain till further orders, Jacob Bingham, Esq." [223]

Figure 39 Burford Drill Shed 1906. The old drill shed used by the Burford Infantry and Cavalry units was donated to the South Brant Agricultural Society. From Edmund Yeigh's property it was moved to the fair grounds to serve as an exhibit building.

Though officially gazetted on September 7, 1866 Jacob Bingham and his troop of men had sought recognition since November 24, 1862. They had also considered amalgamation with another troop that was active in 1862. The following is a letter from Jacob Bingham to the Adjutant General's office:

"*To the Deputy Adj.-General*
Quebec
Sir

We feel very anxious to hear from your department respecting the Cavalry Company of Burford of which you have the list. Mr. Perin has given up any idea of having anything to do with getting up a company of Cavalry or amalgamating with us and says he has written to you to that effect.

I am asked daily by members of the troop if I have heard or gotten any word from headquarters respecting it. Hoping you will reply to this that I may be able to give some answers to the inquiries made. *I have the Honour to be - Sir*

Your obedient servant
Burford *J. Bingham,*
November 24, 1862 [224] *Capt. - Elect.*"

The first officers of the Burford Cavalry were:

Captain Jacob Bingham lived in Bishopsgate village in the Township of Burford. In 1845 he established a foundry that produced agricultural implements such as reapers, mowers and ploughs. In 1857 he was gazetted as Lieutenant in the 1st Oxford Sedentary militia then in 1861 as Captain in the 5th Brant. In 1871 he served as deputy reeve of Burford. Around 1872 as the result of business difficulties, Captain Bingham resigned and left for the United States.

Figure 40 The first meeting of the Burford Volunteer Cavalry Troop was held in the 'Loney and Kirklands' store which was owned for several generations by the Millers then Sprowls of Burford. It is now called the Burford Market located at 118 King Street.

Figure 41 Thomas Lloyd-Jones was the first Cornet of the Burford Troop of Cavalry.

Cornet Thomas Lloyd-Jones was a farmer living in Burford township. He was the son of William and Catherine Lloyd-Jones born in 1840. Thomas at the age of 15 was employed at a mercantile house in Brantford working there for five years. After this, his health being bad, he travelled to England staying two years. After returning he engaged in farming owning 170 acres in 1883. He was a member of the county council for two years, served as Burford reeve, was secretary and treasurer of the Agricultural Society for ten years and was on the board of directors of the County Mutual Insurance company. He married Isabella Miller in 1868 and had four children. He was the first Cornet of the Burford Cavalry Troop.

Two weeks after the Fenian Raid on June 14, 1866 Captain Bingham wrote to the Adjutant General to ensure the awareness that the Burford Cavalry was mustered and ready should they be needed. He also gave a short historical account of his troop saying that the troop had organized and uniformed because of a Circular Letter from the Adjutant General sent on May 19, 1860. [225] They had sent the troop's Service Roll on July 12, 1862 which had been full. A colonel had then visited and inspected them giving a very favourable report. The Brigade Major had also inspected them with a similar favourable report. After the Roll had been sent, the government issued an order to not receive any more troops of cavalry.

Mr. John Thompson of Burford wrote in July 1866, "*the leading men of the west riding of the county of Brant are getting up a petition to present to our members of west Brant to lay before Parliament...to see if justice cans't be done to the Burford troop after being organized for five years.*" [226]

On June 19th the Hon. David Christie wrote to the Adjutant General's office lobbying on behalf of Capt. Bingham's troop: "*I can assure you that they would prove very efficient and I beg strongly to express the wish that they may be accepted.*" [227]

Likewise on August 21st, the Hon. E. B. Wood, MPP, wrote to the Hon. John A. Macdonald, "*permit me to remind you of the promise you made that Jacob Bingham's Cavalry Troop in Burford should be gazetted... The Adj. General said to me he thought the Government could not honourably avoid gazetting this Troop - they having organized, drilled and furnished themselves with clothing on the invitation of the Government.*" [228]

Finally on August 27th , William Little who addressed himself as Secretary of the Burford Cavalry Troop wrote to the Adjutant General saying that Hon. E. B. Wood, MPP, said to him, "*that on account of our having been so long organized, drilled and uniformed that he can get the Company gazetted as a Cavalry Troop.*" [229] Ten days later on September 7, 1866 the troop was officially gazetted as "a special case". According to the Burford historian Squadron Leader (retired) Mel N. W Robertson CD:

"The new Cavalry Troop was organized as Hussars with all the colourful accoutrements of such light cavalry. Their dress consisted of black busbies with white horsetail plumes, dark blue uniforms with gold braid, white sword belts and Spencer carbines. In 1872 the Burford troop became No. 5 Troop of the 2nd Regiment of Cavalry. In September 1882, the 2nd Regiment became the 25th Dragoons and 5th Troop was designated as 'C' Squadron. This designation lasted until March 15th, 1920 when the 25th was made the 10th Dragoons. In 1936, there was a complete reorganization of the militia and the 10th Brant Dragoons were amalgamated with the 2nd Dragoons to form the 2nd/10th Dragoons. Shortly after this amalgamation 'C' Squadron was moved to Brantford." [230]

An officers list is contained in the Addendum on page 110.

The Grand Trunk Railway Companies

The Grand Trunk Railway played an important part in the early development of Canada as it helped open up new parts of the country. It was also an important part of Brantford's local economy because of the men employed and business that it created.

The rail line ran through the centre of Brantford township. It entered on the south-east town line close to the village of Cainsville and took a north-west direction leaving the township north to Paris.

The Brantford station of the Grand Trunk was located where the current station is at the corner of Market and West streets. In the 1860s the company also had several large workshops west of the station between Usher and Pearl streets. In these mechanics were employed building railroad cars and repairing cars and engines. In 1869, 150 men were employed and by 1883, 212. Brantford was the most important station west of Hamilton with four regular daily trains leaving the depot each way along with freight and specials.

Compared to many early businesses, the GTR was very involved in their employees' welfare. The company had a library and literary association with reading room and bath in one of the buildings behind the station. They also sponsored a 30 member fire brigade with fire engine. Associated with their militia companies they had a twenty piece band with both brass and reed instruments.

Although no evidence concerning the militia companies prior to 1866 could be found in official sources, local Brant history says that as early as 1860 an artillery battery was formed in Brantford. The railway had cast a six pounder cannon in their workshops and used it on special occasions. On the celebration of the Prince of Wales' marriage in 1863, the guns boomed early in the morning from current Terrace Hill. The Battery, then called the Railway Artillery Company, marched in the procession to Victoria Square and fired a Royal salute[231].

In 1866 three Grand Trunk Railway rifle companies were organized. The March 1866 Brantford newspaper reported:

"New Volunteer Battalion - The employees on the Grand Trunk have been formed into companies the whole of which make one battalion of volunteers, by order of C. J Brydges, Esq., General Manager of the company." [232]

The Grand Trunk Railway companies in Brantford were gazetted April 27, 1866[233] and were part of a much larger body of troops. The Grand Trunk organized their employees into two Brigades of five Battalions. When most large cities were fielding only several companies it must have been quite a feat to muster 23 rifle companies, 12 artillery batteries and 1 engineer company. Approximately 2,150 men under arms![234]

In a report by Lieut. Col. Galloway he describes the Grand Trunk brigades as follows.

"The value of the organization, extending from Riviere du Loup to Sarnia, Buffalo to Goderich, Richmond to Island Pond, & e., & e., cannot well be over-estimated. Military service being exacted from all men in the Company's employment, a comparatively large force is at all times available, men who, from the discipline maintained in Railway management, inured to danger, in fact the larger portion almost carrying their lives in their hands, cannot fail, with the instructions provided by Government, to make good and steady soldiers, a force (living in the immediate vicinity of the respective headquarters, with armories and magazines at hand) which can be moved with almost the same despatch as regular troops."[235]

The following is the organizational structure of each Brigade. Brantford employees served in the 2nd Brigade 5th Battalion 1st, 2nd and 3rd Company of Rifles.

<u>Grand Trunk Railway Brigade</u> [236]

1st Brigade	2nd Brigade
1st Bn Brigade Garrison Artillery	4th Bn Brigade Garrison Artillery
1 Coy Montreal	1 Coy Toronto
2 Coy Montreal	2 Coy Toronto
3 Coy Montreal	3 Coy Toronto
4 Coy Montreal	4 Coy Toronto
5 Coy Montreal	5 Coy Toronto
6 Coy Montreal	6 Coy Toronto
7 Coy Engineers Montreal	
2nd Bn Grand Trunk Railway Rifles	5th Bn Grand Trunk Railway Rifles
1 Coy Montreal	1 Coy Brantford
2 Coy Montreal	2 Coy Brantford
3 Coy Montreal	3 Coy Brantford
4 Coy Richmond	4 Coy Stratford
5 Coy Sherbrooke	5 Coy St. Marys
6 Coy Point Lewis	6 Coy Sarnia
7 Coy Montreal	7 Coy Sarnia
3rd Bn Grand Trunk Railway Rifles	
1 Coy Montreal	
2 Coy Montreal	
3 Coy Montreal	
4 Coy Brockville	
5 Coy Brockville	
6 Coy Kingston	
7 Coy Belleville	
8 Coy Belleville	
9 Coy Port Hope	

After 1867 the Battalion designations were changed from the original, which is presented here. Brantford's 5th Battalion became the 3rd Battalion.

The First Officers of the 5th Battalion Grand Trunk Railway, Brantford Companies[237]

Major Pillans Stevenson, June 15, 1866

No. 1 Coy, Brantford	
Captain	Thos. Patterson, April 27, 1866
Lieutenant	Hy A. Penfold, May 11, 1866
Ensign	James Barker, May 11, 1866

No. 2 Coy Brantford	
Captain	Chs. Gilbert, April 27, 1866
Lieutenant	Fredk. Lund, May 11, 1866
Ensign	Gowan Clifford, May 11, 1866

No. 3 Coy. Brantford	
Captain	Robert Larmour, April 27, 1866
Lieutenant	Wm. McLean, May 11, 1866
Ensign	Alfred Savage, May 11, 1866

The first record of the activity of the Grand Trunk companies in Brantford is at the Queen's Birthday celebration on May 24th, 1866. The Brantford Expositor recorded that the volunteers were invited and did join in the celebration marching through the streets. [238]

The Grand Trunk companies had their own band and it was said that they were composed mostly of discharged British bandsmen who remained in Brantford when their unit left.

Records in the National Archives also give an indication of the nature of service offered during the Fenian Raid. Official records indicate they guarded bridges and terminals, protected the Grand Trunk Railway line and conducted special railway services at Erie and vicinity.[239]

On November 7, 1866 the Grand Trunk companies conducted a Saturday march around Brantford and the local paper reported on their professional standing after about eight months of existence. They noted, "*we have seldom seen men who have had so few opportunities for drill exhibit more proficiency.*" But along with compliments they also constructively comment, "*we fancy the Grand Trunk men themselves are conscious of it, that they have yet many things to learn.*" [240]

A list of officers is contained in the Addendum on page 111.

Tuscarora Rifle Company

The Tuscarora Rifle Company was gazetted on December 11, 1862.[241] The Captain was William John Simcoe Kerr, commonly called Simcoe Kerr. He was born in 1840, the youngest child of Chief William Johnson Kerr, well-known as leader of the warriors at the Battle of Beaver Dams during the War of 1812, [242] and Elizabeth Brant, daughter of Joseph Brant.

He married Catherine Hunter in 1870 and they moved into the home built by Joseph Brant on Burlington Bay. Simcoe became a lawyer and also served as a reeve of Nelson township. His aunt Catherine, according to Mohawk tradition, named him hereditary chief of the Mohawk succeeding the deceased John Brant. He had the honour of meeting Prince Arthur in 1869 at the door of the Mohawk Chapel during his royal visit. [243]

The Lieutenant was Henry Clinch (Clench), an Oneida chief and a farmer in Ohsweken on Concession 6. He was born and raised in Onondaga Township and married Helen Hess having six children. Lieutenant Clinch had helped lay the cornerstone for Brant's monument. [244]

The Ensign was John Buck, an Onondaga chief. He was deputy speaker of the council for Six Nations in 1892-93 and lived in Tuscarora Township on Concession 5. During Prince Arthur's visit he addressed the Prince in the Mohawk language translated by Chief Johnson. [245] He also stood amongst the honoured guests on the platform during the unveiling of Brant's monument.

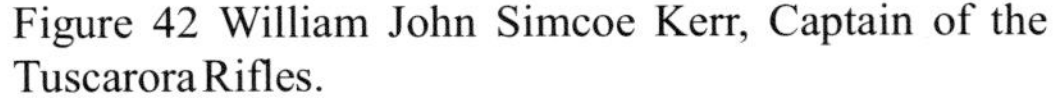

Figure 42 William John Simcoe Kerr, Captain of the Tuscarora Rifles.

Figure 43 Onondaga Chief John Buck was the Ensign of the Tuscarora Rifle Company.

There were no pay lists found in official records but the Service Roll did survive and is as follows:[246]

"Service Roll of the Tuscarora Rifle Company
December 1862
Service Roll of the Rifle company of volunteer militia under the command of William J. S. Kerr. We, whose names are hereunto subscribed, declare that we voluntarily agree to serve in the Rifle company in the township of Tuscarora of volunteer militia, under the conditions of service for the government of the volunteer militia force of Canada, as set forth in the existing militia laws of the province."

Anthony, Albert
Bomfry, George
Buck, Ensign John
Clench, Lieutenant Henry
Croferd, David
David, Joseph
Davis, William
Fish, David
Fraser, Isaac
Gallow, Peter
Garlow, John
Garlow, Philip
Garlow, Phillip C
Givins, David
Green, Abel
House, William
Howlas, Peter
Isaac, Joseph
John, Peter
John, William
Johnson, Isaac
Johnson, Sergeant Joel
Jordan, Nicholis
Joseph, William
Kerr, Captain W. J. Simcoe
Key, George
Key, Peter Senr.
Key, William
Luke, William
Maracle, John
Odor, Henry
Powless, Henry
Powless, Peter
Rankin, Isaac
Rankins, Samual
Ruben, James
Seerling, Jacob
Sky, Charles
Sky, John
Smith, David
Smith, James
Snow, Isaac
Snow, Joseph
Thomas, David
Thomas, Isaac

Green, Daniel	Martin, Adam	Thomas, Torance
Green, George	Maxwell, David	Whiskey, John
Green, William	Monture, Peter	White, George
Harris, John	Newhouse, Peter	Williams, inaen
Henry, John	Nicholas, Rick	Williams, John
Hill, Ezra	Obe, John	Williams, Johnson
Hill, John		

On January 26, 1863 Captain Kerr wrote to headquarters requesting that arms and accoutrements be sent to his home address for convenience and stated that Col. Light had advised him that an inspection wasn't necessary since the company was already gazetted.[247] He received a reply that arms would be sent upon approval of the brigade Major.

He had discussions with Col. Light about a militia unit of battalion strength raised among the Six Nations and the colonel was aggressive in his pursuit of this objective. Captain Kerr prudently suggested waiting to see how the first company worked out. He also suggested that the most important feature for a successful company would be the appointment of good and efficient officers and then proceeded with this cautiously.

The Captain requested that his company be called "Six Nation Warriors". He suggested that this name would add greatly to interest in the Volunteer company within the First Nations community.

Without official explanation, the Tuscarora company was disbanded on April 29, 1864 after about sixteen months of operation.[248]

In 1866 during the Fenian Raid crisis, J. J. Gilkison, the Superintendent of the Indian department tried again to raise a Volunteer company by offering one hundred Six Nations men for service. He wrote to John A. Macdonald then again to the Adjutant General without success. [249]

A list of officers is contained in the addendum on page 111.

Onondaga Rifle Company

The Onondaga Rifle Company was gazetted on February 6, 1863[250] and was one of the companies formed through the initiatives of Dr. Bown MPP for East Brant [251] assisted by Major W. Alger of the 1st Brantford Rifles who was also a resident of Onondaga. [252] The Captain was Matthew Whiting the reeve of Onondaga who for many years was active in municipal politics. He also served as clerk of Number 6 Division Court, as a Justice of the Peace and as County Warden. He was a merchant in business life.

Figure 44 Matthew Whiting was the Captain of the Onondaga Infantry Company.

The Lieutenant was John Waugh. No John Waugh could be found in Onondaga township but he may have been a resident of Oakland township as a general merchant and then a farmer.

The Ensign was Richard Herdsman, Jr. His father, who served for twenty years as Onondaga treasurer, had also served for 31 years in the Kings Guards having fought at the Battle of Waterloo where he had his horse shot out from under him and received four sabre wounds.

Richard Jr. was commissioned as an ensign in the 6th Brant sedentary militia July 1856. His father was a captain. At 37 years of age, Richard Jr. followed in his father's footsteps as a volunteer.

There were no pay lists or a Service Roll found for the Onondaga company and it survived for only fourteen months being officially disbanded on April 29, 1864.[253]

In early 1863 there was also another group of Onondaga men who met for the purpose of organizing a Volunteer company. They went as far as meeting and electing their officers and non-commissioned officers. But there are no official records to indicate they were gazetted by the government. There are no records in Brant county to suggest the company went any further than their initial meeting. This meeting is described later in Chapter 4, "Meeting in Middleport to raise a company."[254]

Newport Infantry Company

The Newport Infantry Company was gazetted on August 31, 1866.[255] This was just after the Fenian Raid scare had calmed down and the excitement of this event would surely have influenced the formation of this unit. The Brantford Expositor reported that

"this company has been officially gazetted. The officers are not yet chosen. We trust that the men will at once endeavour to make themselves thoroughly acquainted with drill and the use of the rifle." [256]

From the very beginning it was envisioned that this company would become a part of the newly gazetted Brant County Infantry Battalion. In the Officers register it is listed as "*No. 7 Co. 38 Brant Battalion*" [257]

The company was very short-lived existing for only four months but it did have some very high level support. The Hon. E. B. Wood MPP for West Riding of Brant had aggressively pursued the official recognition of this company. In a letter to the Hon. John A. Macdonald dated August 27, 1866 he noted,

"two years ago or more at the instance of a circular issued by the Government a company enrolled themselves at Newport, forty-five minute walk from the Town of Brantford, composed almost exclusively of young unmarried men, sturdy fellows, loyal and zealous for the defence of their Queen and Country. Mr. Alger made application more than once to have this company gazetted. But at the time the Government concluded they would not take any more volunteers. Circumstances have now changed."[258]

John A. Macdonald sent the letter to the Adjutant General with a short note dated August 30, 1866 directing that , "*I think you had better have them gazetted at once.*" [259] The company was gazetted the next day but was disbanded on December 14th with the issue of the following General Order.

"Headquarters
General Order *Ottawa, 14 December 1866*
Volunteer Militia
38th 'Brant' Battalion of Infantry
No. 7 Co. Newport
This Company having failed in its organization is hereby removed from the list of the Volunteer Militia." [260]

Drumbo Infantry Company

The Drumbo Infantry Company was a loyal member of the 38th Brant Battalion of Infantry for sixteen years. From the beginning of Brant's Battalion until the end of the non Brantford companies, Drumbo men served in the 38th.

Not much is known of the Drumbo company up to its membership in the Brant Battalion because none of the sources on Brant County have anything to say about Drumbo which is in Oxford County. A few documents were found in the National Archives and are as follows.

On January 22, 1863 the District Brigade Major wrote to the Adjutant General: [261]

"Head Quarters Woodstock
Military District No. 8 January 22, 1863
Sir

I have the honor to enclose a Service Roll of a Company of Volunteer Infantry found at Drumbo in the Township of Blenheim for the satisfaction of His Excellency the Governor General and if approved I would recommend that Wesley Howell, Esquire be appointed as Captain, R. T Hill, Gent. as Lieut. and Charles Andrew Muma, Gent. as Ensign.

I have the honor to be
Sir
Your most obedient servant
W. S Light
Brigade Major No. 8 Military District

Lieut. Col. Walker Powell
Depty. Adj. General of Militia
Quebec"

Enclosed with this letter was the first Service Roll of men:

"Service Roll of the Drumbo Infantry Company, January 1863

Service roll of the 7th battalion Oxford militia of volunteer militia under the command of Capt. Wesley Howell.

We hereunto subscribed, declare that we voluntarily agree to serve in the Drumbo company as Light Infantry of volunteer militia, under the conditions of service for the government of the volunteer militia force of Canada, as set forth in the existing militia laws of the province."

Allen, John
Allison, John
Armstrong, William T.
Bailey, Charles
Collins, Thomas
Cunliffe, Alex
Demar, Cpl. Francis
Dickson, William
Dier, David
Ehle, John
Ferriby, Robert
Frostick, Samuel
Gray, Sgt.---
Gray, W. H.
Greenfield, James
Henderson, Thomas
Hill, Lieut. R. T
Howell, Capt. Wesley
Howell, Henry
Hubbart, Albert
Ireland, Robt.
Levan, Cyrus
Lockhart, Sgt. William
Martin, S.
McBane, John
McCaffey, Tho.
McCarty, Jacob
McCarty, John
Miller, Oliver
Muma, Ensign Charles Andrew
Muma, Jacob
Palmer, John
Pembleton, Al
Regan, B.
Schofield, James
Shannon, Chambers
Simpson, ---
Smith, James E.
Smith, Sgt. Robert
Snyder, P.M.
Stevenson, Cpl. Wm.

The company and officers that were recommended were officially gazetted one week later on January 30, 1863.

Wesley Howell was born in Ancaster, the oldest living child of a family of fourteen. He was raised in Wentworth County and was commissioned in the Wentworth Sedentary militia. He married Emma Vanderlip and had six children.

In early life he acted as Superintendent of his father's manufacturing business for eight years. He then moved to Paris entering into mercantile life for ten years. After this he moved to Blenheim township on Concession 6 Lot 8 about 1 ½ miles east of Drumbo. Here he established a grist and flour mill on the Nith River called Howell's Mills. He remained there for nine years then moved to Brantford. In Brantford he helped establish a company manufacturing starch and vinegar which became the 'British American Starch Works'. In later life he became a successful insurance and real estate agent.

He served as reeve of Brantford Township and as a County councillor for Brant. He was a member of the Masonic, Doric Lodge #121 and Mt. Horeb chapter #21.

The following year a change of officers occurred as reported in the following General Order:

"Headquarters Quebec, 10 June 1864
Volunteer Infantry company Drumbo
To be Lieut.: John Laidlaw, Gentleman, vice Hill, resigned
To be Ensign: James Rodgers, Gentleman, vice Muma, resigned"

In January 1865 Capt. Howell wrote to headquarters to advise that he had filled up his company from forty to its original number of 65 men and requested clothing for them. [262] He also wrote that the men were attending drill once a week.

He received an answer from the Adj. General who stated that it would be difficult to maintain an efficient company if the number of rifles were exceeded and that he not try to increase to 65 men and to maintain his efficiency

The account of Drumbo's part in the Fenian crisis is given in full in Chapter 2. But it should be mentioned that the Drumbo company had the honour of advancing with the military contingent all the way to Fort Erie shore in pursuit of the Fenians.

In 1866 militia fervour was high and many counties formed themselves into battalions for greater efficiency.

Lt. Col. Taylor of the 22nd Battalion Oxford Rifles while organizing his battalion wrote to the Adjutant General: [263]

"In order to promote the efficiency of the 22nd Battalion Oxford Rifles and to complete the organization of that portion of my District I strongly recommend that the infantry companies of 'Drumbo' and 'Ingersoll' be added to the 22nd Battalion."

The Militia Act stated that a battalion must have at least six and no more than ten companies. With the additional two companies Lt. Col. Taylor would have eight companies for his battalion.

Four months later, Taylor's ideas had changed. He then had eleven companies for his 22nd and sought a solution from the Adjutant General: [264]

"I have one company on borders of County Oxford viz. 'Drumbo' (Captain Howell) and as I have a Battalion of ten companies in Oxford I don't know what to do with the Drumbo lads. They would be very handy to form one of the Brant Battalion being on the line of Buffalo and Lake Huron Ry. 6 miles north of Paris. If you can get them into Brant they will make no objection."

So it was that an Oxford County company joined the 38th Battalion of Brant County.

The occupations of members of the Drumbo company are described in the following list:

Lieut. R. T Hill	grocer selling crockery, hardware, wines and liquors.
Ensign C.A. Muma	salesman, brickyard owner.
Ensign James Rogers	blacksmith
Private Almon Peck	carpenter and joiner.
Capt. Wesley Howell	grist and flour mill owner
Private Alex Conliff	stone mason
Private Wm. Lockhart	porter

The Drumbo company remained with the 38th Brant until September 15, 1882 when the Battalion was gazetted as a "City Battalion" at Brantford.[265]

Paylists for several years are added in the Addendum on page 106 and a list of officers on page 111.

105. RGU II C3A3 - 1865, pg 49
106. RG9 1C1 Vol. 136 #1391
107. RG9 1C1 Vol. 136 #1450
108. Militia G. O June 26, 1856
109. RG9 1C1 Vol. 135 #2369
110. The Forks of the Grand, Don Smith, Vol. 1, pg. 293
111. Paris Town Council Minutes: November 3, 1856; April 6, 1857; December 23, 1861
112. Paris Town Council Minutes - Nov. 3, 1856 and Apr. 6, 1857
113. RG9 1C1 Vol. 141 #2757
114. RG8, C Series, Vol. 805, pg. 254-254a
115. RG9 1C1 Vol. 141, #2757
116. RG9 1C1 Vol. 142 #3060
117. Militia General Order, May 16, 1856
118. RG9 1C1 Vol. 146 #3849
119. RG9 1C1 Vol. 146 #3849
120. RG9 1C1 Vol. 147 #4139
121. RG9 1C1 Vol. 148 #4384
122. The Forks of the Grand, Don Smith, Vol. 1, pg. 147
123. RG9 1C1 Vol. 153 #510
124. RG8, C Series, Reel C3361, Vol. 1020, pg. 41
125. Brantford Expositor, May 21, 1858
126. RGU II C3A3 - 1863, pg 53
127. 25 Victoria (S. P. 17) - 1862 The Annual Report on the State of the Militia
128. RGU II C3A3 - 1867, pg 53
129. RG9 1C1 Vol. 237 #2775
130. Militia General Order October 12, 1866
131. Brant County Directory for 1869-70, James Sutherland
132. Brantford Expositor December 23, 1881
133. RGU II C3A3 - 1865, pg 49
134. RG9 1C1 Vol. 163 #258
135. Militia General Order May 19, 1860
136. Brantford Expositor, November 1, 1861
137. RG9 1C1 Vol. 171 #722
138. RG9 1C1 Vol. 171 #722
139. Brantford Council Minutes Vol. 3 January 27, 1862 pg. 191
140. RG9 1C1 Vol. 178 #226
141. RG9 1C1 Vol. 178 #226
142. Thomas C. Cowherd, who owned property on the south side of Colborne Street, opposite the Kerby Hotel in Brantford and Prof. Alexander Graham Bell, the inventor of the telephone, were great chums. On the rear of this property was erected a three-story brick building in which the telephones were manufactured by Bell and Cowherd's son, James H. Cowherd. In his earliest experiments James Cowherd used a common stovepipe wire to run and operate a line between the factory and the Cowherd home and when the telephone became practical Thomas Cowherd and Bell enjoyed daily conversations between their homes.
The Scientific American gave the following account of the death of James H. Cowherd: "The Canadian scientific world will receive with deep regret the intelligence of the death of this rising scientist. Mr. Cowherd died on February 29, 1881, at the early age of 32. He was one of Canada's ablest electricians. At an early age he showed a great taste for constructing mechanical contrivances. Electricity was the field to which he turned. About this time Prof. Bell required a Canadian manufacturer of his telephone and he selected Mr. Cowherd as the most suitable man."
143. F. A. Field, The First Telephone Factory, The Blue Bell, January 1931

144. RG9 1C1 Vol. 180 #546
145. RG9 1C1 Vol. 183 #897
146. RG9 1C1 Vol. 183 #985
147. Brantford Expositor, January 23, 1863
148. RG9 1C1 Vol. 210 #1245
149. Militia General Order January 5, 1865
150. RG9 1C1 Vol. 210 #1245
151. Brantford Expositor, November 10, 1865 and February 2, 1866
152. Brantford Expositor, January 5, 1866 and Grand River Sachem June 27, 1866
153. RGU II C3A3 - 1865, pg 49
154. Brantford Courier 60th Anniversary, December 18, 1899
155. RG9 1C1 Vol. 182 #1160
156. RG9 1C1 Vol. 182 #62 (attached to Vol. 182 #730)
157. RG9 1C1 Vol. 181 #642
158. RG9 1C1 Vol. 182 #730
159. RG9 1C1 Vol. 182 #799
160. RG9 1C1 Vol. 185 #1229
161. RG9 1C1 Vol. 201 #2023
162. RG9 1C1 Vol. 201 #2080
163. RG9 1C1 Vol. 204 #63
164. RG9 1C1 Vol. 209 #1111
165. RG9 1C1 Vol. 213 #1725
166 RGU IIC3A3 - 1865
167 RGU IIC3A3 - 1866
168 RGU IIC3A3 - 1867
169 RG9 1C6, Vol. 20, pg 58
170 Brantford Expositor April 19, 1924 and History of Brant County, Reville, pg 125
171. RG9 1C1 Vol. 213 #1725
172. Sarnia Observer October 28, 1864
173. Brantford Expositor January 13, 1865
174. Sarnia Observer April 7, 1865
175. Sarnia Observer April 14, 1865
176. Brant County Council Minutes December 23, 1865
177. Brantford Expositor December 27, 1864
178. Brantford Expositor December 30, 1864
179. Sarnia Observer March 10, 1865 and March 17, 1865
180. Sarnia Observer February 17, 1865
181. Brantford Expositor February 10, 1865
182. Brantford Expositor February 10, 1865
183. Brantford Expositor March 24, 1865
184. Brantford Expositor January 27, 1865
185. Sarnia Observer March 31, 1865
186. Sarnia Observer May 5, 1865
187. Brantford Expositor, April 14 and April 28 1865
188. Brantford Expositor, May 5, 1865
189. Brantford Expositor, January 13, 1865
190. Brantford Expositor, July 20, 1866
191. Brantford Expositor, Sept. 14 and Sept. 21, 1866
192. Brantford Expositor January 18, 1867 & February 1, 1867
193. 27 Victoria (S. P. No. 13) -1864 and Brantford Expositor Aug. 7 and Sept. 4, 1863
194. RGU IIC3A3 - 1867, pg 54
195. Brantford Courier June 9, 1866
196. Brantford Courier June 9, 1866
197. RG9 1C1 Vol. 230 #900
198. Brantford Council Minutes November 26, 1866
199. RGU 11C3A3, -1863, pg 55
200. RG9 1C1 Vol. 207 #63
201. RG9 1C1 Vol. 192 #207
202. The History of the County of Brant, Warner & Beers, pg. 515
203. RG9 1C1 Vol. 212 #1632
204. Brantford Expositor October 16, 1863
205. RG9 1C1 Vol. 212 #1632
206. RG9 1C1 Vol. 214 #1950
207. RG9 1C1 Vol. 212 #1632
208. The Early Political and Military History of Burford, R. C. Muir pg. 370
209. RG9 1C6 Vol. 20, pg. 253

210. RG9 1C6 Vol. 20, pg. 303
211. RGU II C3A3 - 1867, pg 17
212. Brantford Expositor December 10, 1927
213. Brantford Expositor August 24, 1866
214. RG9 1C1 Vol 233 #1674
215. RG9 1C1 Vol 233 #1674
216. RG9 1C1 Vol 233 #1739
217. RG9 1C1 Vol 233 #1674
218. RG9 1C1 Vol 233 #1674
219. RG9 1C1 Vol. 233, #1739
220. The Early Political and Military History of Burford, R. C. Muir, pg. 363
221. The Early Political and Military History of Burford, R. C. Muir, pg. 362
222. Brantford Expositor, May 18, 1883
223. Brantford Expositor September 14, 1866
224. RG9 1C1 Vol 187 #1569
225. RG9 1C1 Vol 231 #1266
226. RG9 1C1 Vol 233 #1775
227. RG9 1C1 Vol 231 #1325
228. RG9 1C1 Vol 235 #2190
229. RG9 1C1 Vol 235 #2190
230. Burford's Military History, Squadron Leader (retired) Mel Robertson CD
231. Brantford Expositor, May 25, 1860 and The Greater Brantford Expositor 1907, pg. 95
232. Brantford Expositor March 23, 1866
233. RGU II C3A3 - 1867, pg 21
234. 31 Victoria, (S. P. 35) - 1867 Annual Report on the State of the Militia
235. 31 Victoria, (S. P. 35) - 1867 Annual Report on the State of the Militia
236. RG9 II F6 Vol. 265-266
237. RGU II C3A3 - 1867, pg 68
238. Brantford Expositor May 25, 1866
239. RG9 II A5, Vol. 3, pg. 39, 169, 170, 213-216
240. Brantford Expositor November 7, 1866
241. RGU II C3A3 - 1863, pg 54
242. Burlington - Memories of Pioneer Days, Dorothy Turcotte, pg. 25-26
243. The History of Brant County, Reville, pg. 201
244. The History of Brant County, Reville, pg. 56
245. The History of Brant County, Reville, pg. 201
246. RG9 1C1 Vol. 190, #1958
247. RG9 1C1 Vol. 190, #1958
248. RG9 1C6 Vol. 19, pg. 307
249. RG9 1C1 Vol. 231 #1196 and Vol. 235 #2147
250. RG9 1C6 Vol. 19, pg. 396
251. RG9 1C1 Vol. 207 #63
252. RG9 1C1 Vol. 207 #63 and Brantford Expositor January 23, 1863
253. RG9 1C6 Vol. 19, pg. 396
254. Brantford Expositor March 6, 1863
255. RG9 1C1 Vol. 235 #2326
256. Brantford Expositor September 7, 1866
257. RG9, 1C6, Vol. 20, Register of Officers, 1862-1869, Table of Contents (under Newport)
258. RG9 1C1 Vol. 235 #2326
259. RG9 1C1 Vol. 235 #2326
260. Militia General Order December 14, 1866
261. RG9 1C1 Vol. 191 #167
262. RG9 1C1 Vol. 216 #79
263. RG9 1C1 Vol. 131 "1866 letters"
264. RG9 1C1 Vol. 236 #2690
265. Brantford Expositor December 23, 1881

Chapter 4

INQUIRIES AND OFFERS REGARDING SERVICE

This chapter is a collection of documents describing offers to form units, inquiries about forming units and units that were organized and fully operational yet not officially gazetted by the government.

From these documents it can be seen that though there were few militia units officially authorized in this early period it was not for lack of enthusiasm by the citizens of Brant.

Offer to Raise a Unit of Infantry/Cavalry at Burford, 5 August 1856

In a letter to Col. Askin who commanded the military district, Lt. Col. C. S Perley asked what assistance the government would give in arms and equipment. He stated that the 5th Brant Sedentary militia had a strong desire to organize a volunteer company. As commanding officer of a sedentary battalion he was concerned that a volunteer company would improve his battalion and strengthen esprit de corps. [266]

The Adjutant-General's Office advised that they could furnish arms but the company must uniform themselves.

On 10 March 1857 Lt. Col. Perley submitted a Service Roll for the proposed company that would be raised within the limits of his battalion. [267]

"Proposed Service Roll of the Burford Volunteer Rifle Company March 1857"

Benns, George	Henderson, Joseph	Postle, William
Berry, John	Henderson, Samuel	Ramsey, James H.
Brown, George	Heywood, Joseph	Robertson, William
Brown, Robert	Johnson, William	Rutherford, John
Evans, L. Walter	Jones, Capt. Joseph	Simmons, G.
Findlay, Robert	Jones, Stephen	Smiley, J. H.,
Flewelling, Samuel	Lester, John N.	Smith, James
Flewelling, W. W	Lightly, George	Smith, William
Forsythe, H.	Little, Lieut. William	Tillison, Joseph
Fowler, George H.	McCaffry, Edward	Wetmore, B.F.
Fowler, John W.	Miller, Ensign Franklin	Wetmore, John
Harris, James G.	Mills, G.	Wetmore, Stephen H.
Hearne, George	Mitchell, Thomas	Wood, George
Hearne, James	Munger, J.	Wooden, David
Hearne, William	Murray, Charles	Wooden, Ira C.
Henderson, Alexander	Murray, Jas.	Wooden, William H.
Henderson, James S.	Postle, Henry	Zacher, John

On April 29, 1857 Lt. Col. Perley again wrote to the Adjutant-General. He had been told that he could not get rifles so he asked if the company could have percussion muskets and be styled a light infantry company. He advised that the men didn't expect any pay for uniforms or drill. A second Service Roll was submitted with many of the names being identical to the first.[268]

"Proposed 2nd Service Roll of the Burford Light Infantry Company April 1857

We the undersigned yeomanry of the township of Burford, County of Brant, do hereby agree to form ourselves into a Volunteer Light Infantry Company under the provisions of the present Militia Act for Upper Canada and to conform to all the rules and regulations of said Act.

We further agree and pledge ourselves to uniform ourselves at our own expense and to learn our discipline as may be prescribed by the provisions of said Act, in relation to Volunteer Light Infantry companies for Upper Canada."

Brown, George
Flewelling, ---
Flewelling, I. B.
Forsyth, _C.
Fowler, George H.
Green, Cornelius
Harris, James
Hearne, George
Hearne, William
Henderson, A.
Henderson, Ensign Alexander
Henderson, James S.
Henderson, Joseph
Heyward, Joseph
Jones, Capt. Joseph
Jones, Stephen
Lightly, George
Little, Lieut. William
Mills, Isaac
Munger, James
Murray, James
Ramsey, James H.
Rutherford, John
Simmons, W.F.
Smiley, John
Wetmore, B.F.
Wetmore, John
Wetmore, Stephen H.
Wood, George
Wooden, ---
Wooden, I. C
Zucker, John

On May 11, 1857 William Little, the proposed Lieutenant, wrote to the Adjutant-General asking why the request to raise a volunteer company had been denied. [269] Lt. Col. Perley had initially said they could raise a company but opposed it and then had advised the men they couldn't. Little hadn't completely believed Perley and wanted the Adjutant-General to tell him directly that they couldn't raise a company. Lt. Col. Perley had given as a reason that the British government was going to make the Canadian government pay for the arms therefore the government was not giving out any more. But the men were seeing other companies gazetted in other places and they wanted to hear why their offer was declined, directly from the Adjutant-General. Lastly he made an offer to raise a cavalry troop instead of infantry if it would be accepted.

In reply Little was told that rifles were not being supplied free anymore.

On May 29, 1861 William Little wrote again to the Adjutant-General. [270]

"About the 8th of May 1857 I sent you a communication...Having thus failed we have thought of organizing a company of Cavalry...Those forming the company will furnish their own regimental clothing and wish to know what assistance will be rendered by the government."

The answer was as follows: *"No assistance of any kind can be granted by government but if the Corps will organize an effort might be made to give them swords and belts."*

On June 14, 1861 Little wrote *"we have met and agreed to organize, uniform and maintain the company referred to in my last provided the government supply the members with swords and belts as you stated in your communication."* [271]

Little asked if they could choose their own officers and how many men would be allowed in the company. As of June 1861 they had about forty members.

On February 13, 1862, for the first time, the elected Captain James Munger wrote to the Adjutant-General in place of William Little: *"I have the honour to acknowledge the receipt of your letter to Wm. Little."* He enclosed the Service Roll for the cavalry troop as follows: [272]

"Service Roll of the Brant County Troop of Cavalry -to be stationed at the Village of Clairmont, January 1862"

Ballard, H. A
Byrne, Claudius
Cairns, James Jr.
Herrett, ---
Heywood, David
Hood, John
Meadows, Walter
Munger, Capt. James
Perrin, Thomas

Clark, William	Jacksons, Joseph H.	Simkes, William T.
Doyle, James	Jillian, Joseph	Smith, Cornet Benjamin
Dutcher, Ephraim	Kelly, Adam	Wardell, Cyrus
Eddy, John	Lewis, William	Watts, F.
Fish, John	Little, Adjutant William	Wetmore, Stephen H.
Flewelling, Thomas G.	Marshall, Lieut. William	White, Amand B.
Fowler, Alexander	McAlister, John	Willard, Tige
Hanmer, David	McWilliams, A. B	Wilson, Surgeon MD, Geo. D.
Hanmer, James		

Munger stated that twenty men had furnished uniforms at their own expense. Many more would enrol but could not afford the uniform.

The uniforms for the troop were custom made in Brantford by the Strobridge and Botham Company. They were of dark blue cloth, trimmed with white for the men and silver for the officers. The jacket was of a short shell design and the pants were also blue with one wide white stripe down them. The headdress was made by Mr. Silas Butters a Colborne Street hat maker. They were of the same blue cloth with white band and straight leather peak. [273]

No official record of the company being authorized could be found but Muir wrote that the Minister of Militia unofficially authorized the troop. They drilled alternately in Burford, Bishopsgate and Mount Vernon.

After Captain Munger moved away in 1864, Muir wrote that the troop practically ceased to exist.

Offer to raise an Artillery unit May 23, 1857 Geo. Mathew, Brantford

The following letter from a Brantford resident expressed an early interest in forming an artillery battery: [274]

"Brantford C. W. May 23rd 1857

Sir

I am requested by several parties residing here to communicate with you in regard to raising a Volunteer Artillery Company. It is understood that there is no letter A (Class A) *Rifle companies to be obtained, it is therefore desirable to raise an Artillery Company. Please have the kindness to afford us the necessary information in regard to the organization of said company, and what the government will do in the way of providing arms, accoutrements, clothes, guns horses and etc.*

I have the honor Sir to be your obedient servant

Geo. Mathew

Col. Baron DeRottenburg
Adjutant Genl. Militia
Toronto"

The response to Mathew was as follows:

"...there are no means at the disposal of H. Majesty to arm any more volunteers Corps. Of Artillery..."

Offer to Raise a Corps of 300 to 500 men for Service in India, Oct. 24, 1857

Adjutant of the 2nd Brant Battalion, William Morgan, Brantford

Adjutant Morgan wrote to the Adjutant-General advising that he had numerous applications from young men to serve in India during the Indian Mutiny. Morgan was at a loss as to what to say so he made an offer to the government that if permission was given to open a depot, then in a few weeks 300 to 500 men could be raised for service in India.

He regretted that his business and family situation prevented him from personally going to India but that he would serve his country in the way mentioned if authorized. [275] Brant history mentions no recruit depot being established.

The Brantford Philharmonic offers a Company for Service, January 7, 1858

B. Hazelhurst, Brantford

The local band called the Brantford Philharmonic Band became interested in forming a volunteer company, wrote to the Adjutant-General and went as far as sending a Service Roll. The following is the letter and Roll. [276]

"Brantford January 7th, 1858

Baron De Rottenburg, C. B.

My Lord Baron,

Enclosed I submit now a list of names of the Brantford Philharmonic Band who are desirous of being formed into a Rifle Company. Our Band has been organized nearly two years, and wear the Rifle Brigade uniform and are in a state of good proficiency as a Band. They had the honor of assisting in the escort of His excellency the administrator of the Government at the late Provincial Fair. The band most respectfully request, if possible, that you would place them in Class "A" and would also refer now to Major Nickenson of your city, and adjutant Morgan, 2nd Battalion Brant as to our respectability and the estimation we are held in by the public.

I have the honor to be respectfully yours

B. Hazelhurst
Leader B. P. Band"

"Proposed Service Roll of the Brantford Philharmonic Band, January 1858"

Beck, T.	Latham, S.	Strobridge, A.
Biddle, T.	McBrien, I.	Thompson, I.
Digby, A.	Ormrod, Wm.	Totten, W.
Gilkison, T.	Penfold, A.	Usher, A.
Hazelhurst, B.	Racey, Henry - for Capt.	VanBrocklin, B.F.
Holmes, G.	Saddler, W.	White, F.
Hunter, Wm.	Smith, A.	Whitham, Wm.
Kelk, W.	Smith, C. E.	Winterbotham, B.

The Adjutant-General's response to the offer of service was that there were no vacancies in Class "A" and that the minimum number for a company is 50 members.

Brantford #2 Fire Company Inquires about raising a company, May 30, 1861

A.W. Smith, Brantford

One letter to the Adjutant-General's office shows an interest by one of the fire companies of Brantford. [277]

"Brantford, May 30th 1861

Lt. Col. Donald McDonald
Dep. Adj. General U. C.

Dear Sir

I would respectfully beg to ask you if a Fire Company should desire to be enrolled as a military company whether the government would do anything for them in the way of furnishing arms, clothing, drill sergeant etc.

An answer at your convenience would much oblige.
I have the honor to be
Sir
Your obt. Servant
A. W. Smith
Foreman Fire Co. No. 2"

The response appears as the following notations made at the bottom of the letter:

"Nothing of any kind could be given but percussion muskets and accoutrements, old pattern - and the company could only be in Class B. --R. B."

Offer to raise a troop of cavalry, November 19, 1861, Capt. George Racey, Brantford

Lt. Col. James Wilkes, commanding officer of the 2nd Brant Battalion Sedentary militia wrote to the Adjutant-General's office reminding them that in 1859 he had written on behalf of one of his officers, Capt. George Racey, who wished to raise a troop of cavalry in Branford. In 1859, Racey was answered that there were no arms available and therefore the offer of service could not be accepted.

Wilkes reaffirmed Racey's request to raise a troop of cavalry and recommended him for consideration. [278]

Request for a commission to raise a company in Brantford, October 8, 1861, A. Mathews

A. Mathews wrote to the Adjutant-General stating that since a volunteer company had been removed from the list of the Active Force then he would like to apply for a commission to organize a company in Class "A". [279]

Offer to raise a troop of cavalry in Brantford, December 9, 1861, Ensign David Curtis

Lt. Col. A. Bunnell, commanding officer of the 1st Brant Battalion wrote to the Adjutant-General's office advising them that Ensign David Curtis of his battalion of sedentary militia would like to organize a troop of cavalry in Brantford. Bunnell asked for permission to do this and inquired about the equipment to be provided by the government. [280]

Inquiry about forming a battery of artillery, November 22, 1861, Capt. George S. Wilkes

Capt. Wilkes wrote to the Adjutant-General's office respecting the formation of a field battery of artillery. He advised that he, being the senior captain in the 1st Brant Battalion, wished to know the best way of applying and if recommendations were needed. [281]

About two weeks later Lt. Col. Bunnell wrote to the Adjutant General giving Capt. Wilkes an excellent recommendation regarding the organization of a field battery. [282]

There was no record found of any field batteries organized in Brant at this time.

Meeting in Middleport to raise a company, March 6, 1863, Brantford Expositor [283]

"The members of the Volunteer Infantry Company of Middleport, on Friday evening Feb 27th, met for the purpose of electing officers for said company.

Moved by J. W. Butter, seconded by Robt. Wade that Robert McLaran, Esq., take the chair - carried.

Moved by W. B. Fyfe, seconded by R. Wade that N. Mariet, be appointed Secretary - carried.

The chairman briefly stated the object of the meeting and concluded by complimenting the people of Middleport and vicinity for the ready manner in which they responded to the call of the government and further hopes to see the Middleport Volunteer infantry company second to none in Canada.

Moved by W. B. Fyfe, seconded by Benjamin Daugherty, jnr, that Robert Wade, Esq., be elected Captain. There being no further nominations the chairman declared R. Wade, Esq. unanimously elected.

Moved by W. B. Fyfe, seconded by Fred Nicholson that H. Nichols be elected Lieutenant - in amendment by R. Math seconded by J. W. Butter, that N. Ma-- be elected -Ma. M-- declining in favour of Mr. H. Nichols who was duly declared elected.

Moved by A. Ludlow, seconded by W. B. Fyfe that Bridar Howell, be elected Ensign - in amendment by Wm. Flemming, seconded by James Hager, that James McArthur be elected Ensign. The former was declared elected by the casting vote of the chairman.

Messrs. N. Monet, Lewis Dennis and Adam Mitchell were elected Sergeants and Charles Jennings, John Dalton and Edgar Walker were elected Corporals.

Liberal sums were at once offered, headed by the Captain for the purpose of erecting a permanent Drill room and on motion it was agreed to meet on Thursday at 8 o'clock a.m. for the purpose of removing a building to a more convenient site and to take immediate steps to build an addition to the building making a room about 25 to 60 feet. The meeting adjourned about 10 o'clock it being fully agreed that the movement was thus far, decidedly successful."

The above article from the Branford Expositor described the first meeting of a proposed volunteer company. There is no evidence that the company was ever officially gazetted nor is there a record of the company or the proposed drill shed in Brant county history.

Articles about a third existing militia company in Brantford, March 6, 1863, Capt. Curtis

The following is an article about an unofficial infantry company existing in Brantford at the same time the 1st and 2nd Brantford rifle companies existed.

"The 1st Brant Infantry Co. - Capt. Curtis' Infantry Co., now meet twice weekly in the drill room for exercise. This will, from present appearances, ultimately be one of the finest companies in the country. It is composed for the most part of fine soldierly looking men, and they all enter with spirit into the drill exercises and hence it will take but a short time for them to become as expert in company exercise as the two rifle companies of the town." [284]

Another document that relates to a third militia company existing in Brantford is the following from Brantford's council minutes, 1862.

"Mr. Quinlan gave notice that two months from date he will ask for the sum of two thousand dollars for the purpose of raising a military uniform for the three rifle companies now organized in this town." [285]

These two documents indicate a third company in existence at this time in Brantford that was not gazetted by the government.

Offer to raise a unit of artillery/cavalry at Mt. Pleasant, January 31, 1863, Dr. A. H. Cooke

Dr. A. H. Cooke of Mount Pleasant wrote,

"The Militia fever is very high in this part of the country just now."

He reminded the Adjutant-General that there was already an infantry company in Mt. Pleasant and stated that there were many who would like to start an artillery battery. Dr. Cooke asked several questions about establishing a battery and stated that there would be no difficulties in getting a respectable battery that would do honor to the country. [286]

In answer to the inquiry the Adjutant-General replied,

"thanks for offer but at present His Excellency the Commander in Chief declines to accept services of any new companies of volunteer artillery."

On March 13, 1866, after the Fenian Raid mobilization that month, Dr. Cooke again wrote to the Adjutant-General advising that he had a son who had just returned from the U.S. army having served several years as a cavalry officer under General Sheridan. Cooke advised that his son, William Winer Cooke, had excellent references and had been wounded in the U.S. Civil War at the Battle of Petersburgh and would like to raise a cavalry troop in Mt. Pleasant or to be considered for service against the Fenians. Numerous applications were being made by young men to his son to organize a troop for active service. [287]

William Winer Cooke was a good friend of U.S. General George Armstrong Custer. In the next document W. W Cooke wrote to the Adjutant-General.

Offer of a troop of cavalry at Mount Pleasant, August 6, 1866, W. W Cooke

The following is a letter from W. W Cooke to the Adjutant-General:

"Mount Pleasant C. W.
August 6th, 1866

Walker Powell
Lt. Col. & Dep. Adjt. Genl.
Sir

I have the honor to report that I have organized a troop of Cavalry in this place. They are properly enrolled on official Muster Rolls. The men are with very few exceptions persons of good standing in surrounding country and are very anxious that the Government acknowledge them. If you should obtain permission for me to go on with the troop I shall put them at once under a course of drill. Hoping to hear from you at your earliest convenience.

I remain
Your Obdt. Servant
W. W Cooke" [288]

Mohawk P. O
C. West

Three months after this letter W. W Cooke had received a commission in the U.S. 7th Cavalry. During his career he obtained the honor of becoming a brevet Lieutenant-Colonel and adjutant of the regiment. His death came with Custer at the Battle of the Little Big Horn commonly known as 'Custer's Last Stand'. His military career is detailed more fully by Arnold and French in Custer's Forgotten Friend, The Life of W. W Cooke.

Offering a company for immediate service during Fenian Crisis, June 6, 1866

James McLean, Justice of the Peace, Mt. Pleasant

The following letter to the Adjutant-General sent immediately after the Fenian Raid offered a company to go at any moment for service. [289]

"Mount Pleasant 6th June, 1866

Col. P. L. MacDougall
Adjutant General

Dear Sir

On the 19th of March last or about the time we were threatened with invasion by a party called Fenians, I called a Public meeting for the purpose of organizing a company of volunteers. Members put their names down and expressed their willingness to go at any moment and repel the foe if they should invade Canada.

At that time the government did not require any more volunteers. However the company met for drill several evenings and would have continued to drill but we were informed that the government would not send us a drill instructor.

If you will allow me to get up a company and furnish us with clothing and arms I will attend to it immediately hoping you will reply immediately.

And oblige
Yours truly

James McLean, J. P

PS Address
James McLean, Mount Pleasant P. O.
via Port Hope C. M."

---

266. RG9 1C1 Vol. 138 #1810
267. RG9 1C1 Vol. 142 #3047
268. RG9 1C1 Vol. 144 #3420
269. RG9 1C1 Vol. 144 #3483
270. RG9 1C1 Vol. 168 #270
271. RG9 1C1 Vol. 169 #320
272. RG9 1C1 Vol. 181 #653
273. Brantford Expositor, Sept. 5, Oct. 11, 1861; and The Early Political and Military History of Burford, R. C. Muir, Hurley Printing, 1913, pg. 310.
274. RG9 1C1 Vol. 145 #3554
275. RG9 1C1 Vol. 118 #4328
276. RG9 1C1 Vol. 149 #19
277. RG9 1C1 Vol. 168 #271
278. RG9 1C1 Vol. 171 #707
279. RG9 1C1 Vol. 171 #609
280. RG9 1C1 Vol. 176 #1163
281. RG9 1C1 Vol. 171 #705
282. RG9 1C1 Vol. 175 #1133
283. Brantford Expositor, March 6, 1863
284. Brantford Expositor, March 6, 1863
285. Brantford Council Minutes, January 27, 1862
286. RG9 9 IC1 Vol. 192 #295
287. RG9 9 IC1 Vol. 227 #270
288. RG9 9 IC1 Vol. 234 #1954
289. RG9 9 IC1 Vol. 230 #1098

Chapter 5

FORMING THE 38TH BRANT BATTALION OF INFANTRY

After the Militia Act of 1859[290] groups of companies began joining together to form battalions. At this time the Hon. John A. Macdonald was emphasizing that

"it was of great importance that the Volunteer companies should be trained to act in battalions." [291]

Macdonald was stating something that quite simply made sense. The threats to Canada at that time, if they came, were believed to be on a scale that would require a force larger than the company to be manoeuvred on the battlefield and men needed to be trained and ready to deter this enemy. The next step was a unit of battalion strength and this was pursued to train the officers and men to work together as a larger force.

In 1866 a whole series of counties such as Halton, Middlesex, Norfolk and many others along with Brant began to form battalions.[292]

In Brant's case the 38th Brant Battalion of Infantry was gazetted on September 28, 1866. In the local newspaper the Battalion was announced as follows:

"Brant Battalion: We are much pleased to notice by the Canada Gazette, of Saturday the 13th inst. that Major Patton has been appointed Lt. Colonel of the Brant Battalion. We have no doubt this appointment will give general satisfaction, as Lieut. Col. Patton is an efficient officer." [293]

In the official Militia General Orders the appointment of the commanding officer read as follows:

"Headquarters

Ottawa, 12 Oct. 1866

Volunteer Militia

38th "Brant Battalion of Infantry'
To be Lieut.-Colonel acting till further orders:
Major William Patton
The numbering of the companies of the
Battalion will be as follows viz.:

No. 1 Company,	*Paris Rifle*	*co.*
No. 2	*1st Brantford*	*do*
No. 3	*2nd do*	*do*

and not as was heretofore stated in
general order No. 5 of the 28th Sept., last."

As early as January 1863 Lt. Col. James Wilkes, commanding officer of the 2nd Brant Battalion Sedentary Militia was thinking ahead about battalion size unit organizations. He offered himself to command a new volunteer battalion in Brant County. The following is the letter offering his services. [294]

"Brantford January 28th, 1863

Sir

As there are now formed and in course of formation several Volunteer companies in this County, I beg to make application for the command of the Battalion if it is the intention of His Excellency the Commander in Chief to have the companies brought together hereafter for Battalion drill.

Lt. Col. Walker Powell
D. A General of Militia
Quebec

Sir
I have the honor to be
Your Obd. Servant
James Wilkes, Lt. Col. 2nd Batl. Brant Militia"

Major William N. Alger of the 1st Brantford Rifles in 1864 had also written to the Adjutant-General putting forward the case for forming a Battalion with himself as commanding officer. [295]

In 1866 Capt. William Patton formerly Captain of the Paris Rifles was made commanding officer of the new Brant Battalion.

Figure 45 Lieut. Col. William Patton was the first Commanding Officer of the 38th Brant Battalion of Infantry.

One of the first duties of the new 38th Battalion was to attend a training course at Thorold which was established to give the new battalions instruction. The camp also was intended to provide a measure of protection for the Niagara frontier as once or twice Fenians had been reported to be gathering on the American side of the Niagara river.[296]

The first camp of instruction began mid August 1866 and continued for seven weeks ending October 6th . The battalions changed about every week with several attending at a time. In total over 6,000 NCO's and 475 officers were trained that year.[297]

The camp staff were Commandant: Col. Garnet Wolseley, Brigade Major and Company Quartermaster: Lt. Col. Jarvis, Acting Aide-de-Camp: Lt. Col. Houltoin and Company Paymaster: Major Alger (formerly of the 1st Brantford Rifles and an Onondaga resident.)[298]

Brant County's six companies arrived September 22nd with twenty officers , 46 NCO's, and 250 Privates. Lt. Col. William Patton the new Commanding Officer led and trained the men in battalion drill.[299]

Two other battalions trained at Thorold with the 38th Brant, the 32nd Bruce and a provisional battalion of six companies from the area south of Brant County.[300]

The local paper ran a humorous article about the trip to Thorold. Apparently a patriotic merchant at Hamilton was aware the Dundas infantry was to pass through Hamilton station and sent a messenger with a case of biscuits, cheese and refreshments for them. Upon arriving at the station the boy seeing the men of Brant in their red coats, delivered the items and left. The men apparently neglected to mention who they were and devoured the food in a hurry. Or perhaps the boy forgot to ask.[301]

The typical camp of instruction[302] would have had long rows of bell tents suitable for ten to twelve men each which were quarters during training. Latrines would be dug and field kitchens constructed. Field equipment, such as cooking utensils, would be loaned from imperial stores or the battalions asked to bring their own. An adequate water supply, an extensive flat plain for the encampment and a large open area close by for battalion and brigade drill were characteristic of the camp.

When the recruits arrived they would be issued a couple of blankets, a bolster case (mattress case) and enough straw to fill it. They would then be assigned to a tent. Meals were nourishing but not extravagant. The traditional pound of bread and pound of beef was served with vegetables and a few ounces of tea, sugar and salt. If the battalion commanding officer was generous he might supply some extras at his own expense.

The camp routine adhered to was the same as Her Majesty's regiments. The hours of reveille, meals, parades and tattoo varied little. Five hours of drill in squad, company, skirmishing and battalion formations was practised each day.

Morning parade	6:30 to 7:30 a.m.
Forenoon parade	10:00 a.m. to Noon
Afternoon parade	3:00 to 5:00 p.m.

The men would participate in the usual camp duties such as mounting guards, sentry and field officer responsibilities.

Also traditional was the march to the ranges to fire thirty rounds then trudge back to camp.

The one exception to this routine was Sunday when the men would have church parade with the choice of attending the Roman Catholic or Protestant services.

At some camps the YMCA opened a booth in the camp where religious services were held in the evening. They also supplied the men with newspapers, pens, ink and paper free of charge.

The number of days spent in camp would vary each year in relation to how much money the government had set aside for camp training. In 1866, the first camp was seven days long for each battalion.

Figure 46 Camp at Thorold 1866

On their arrival home from camp the men were met at the station by citizens of Brantford and heartily applauded. Preceded by their band, they marched to Market Square and were dismissed. Now they were certified trained as a battalion.[303]

As soon as possible after returning from camp Lt. Col. Patton called a meeting of all volunteer officers of the county at Brantford to discuss issues.

Foremost was the selection of staff officers. It was tradition in the militia that the senior officer would be given the senior position and Lt. Col. Patton himself was the most senior volunteer officer. The problems that arose were some officers threatening to resign if a particular officer was made battalion major or adjutant. The internal politics of the militia unit came to the surface as Patton tried to find solutions. [304] Lt. Col. Patton's decision on key staff appointments is contained in the following list of officers:[305]

<u>38th Brant Battalion of Infantry</u>

Lt. Colonel:	William Patton Nov. 20, 1867
Major:	Hiram Dickie Nov. 30.1866
Paymaster:	William Grant Nov. 30, 1866 - Sept. 6, 1867 (Resigns)
	Andrew Morton Sept. 6, 1867
Adjutant:	Samuel W. Fear Nov. 30, 1866 - Feb. 28, 1868 (Resigns)
	David Spence D. I Feb. 28, 1868
Quartermaster:	Francis Grenny Sept. 6, 1867
Surgeon:	Edwin Theodore Bown MD Jan. 25, 1867
Assistant Surgeon:	Duncan Marquis MD Dec. 13, 1867

At the time the independent companies joined together to form the 38th Battalion several of the old company commanders had been given staff appointments. This allowed for promotions and at the formation of the battalion the seven companies with captains were as follows:[306]

COMPANY #	COMPANY	CAPTAIN
1	Paris Rifles	Baird, Andrew H.
2	1st Brantford Rifles	Curtis, David
3	2nd Brantford Rifles	Inglis, J. J.
4	Mt. Pleasant Infantry	Heaton, Crosley
5	3rd Brantford Infantry	Lemmon, Henry
6	Burford Infantry	Yeigh, Edmund
7	Drumbo Infantry	Laidlaw, John

#7 Company was originally the Newport Infantry Company but when it failed in its organization the Drumbo company was substituted.[307]

The independent companies history came to an end in 1866 when the 38th Brant Battalion was formed.

The "38th" or 'Duffs' (an abbreviation of Dufferin which refers to the 38th's first Honorary Colonel, The Earl of Dufferin.) as they affectionately became known, continued gaining an honourable reputation through the years.

Figure 47 The old Alexandra Park drill shed served as drill hall and meeting place for Brant's 38th Battalion. (Photo taken in 1883.)

Brant County's current militia has a new regimental designation but the same spirit that inspired early Brant residents to join together in the cause of freedom and peace still inspires today's generation to go to the ends of the earth in pursuit of these ideals.

A detailed table of the reorganizations, conversions, redesignations and amalgamations from the original volunteer companies to the present 56th Field Regiment, Royal Canadian Artillery, is included in the addendum on page 132.

290. 22 Victoria, Ch 18, Sec 15, 1859, An Act to amend and make permanent the laws relating to the militia of this province
291. Brantford Expositor, July 20, 1866
292. Canada's Soldiers, George Stanley, pgs 213-214
293. Brantford Expositor, October 26, 1866
294. RG9 1C1 Vol. 192 #278
295. RG9 1C1 Vol. 207 #63
296. Canada's Soldiers, George Stanley, pgs 228 and 31 Victoria (S. P. No. 35) - 1867, pg 3-4, The Annual Report on the State of the Militia
297. Muir, R. C., The Military History of Burford, pg 313
298. Muir, R. C., The Military History of Burford, pg 370
299. 31 Victoria (S. P. No. 35) - 1867, The Annual Report on the State of the Militia
300. 31 Victoria (S. P. No. 35) - 1867, The Annual Report on the State of the Militia
301. Brantford Expositor, September, 28, 1866
302. D. Morton, A Military History of Canada, pg 95-96 and 29 Victoria (S. P. No. 4) - 1866, The Annual Report on the State of the Militia
303. Brantford Expositor, October 5, 1866
304. RG9 1C1 Vol. 237 #2871
305. RG9 1C6, Vol 20, pg 58
306. RGU II C3A3 - 1867, pg 53-54
307. Militia General Order December 14, 1866

ADDENDUM

Abbreviations

Arty.	Artillery	Gen.	General
Capt.	Captain	G. O.	General Order
Cav.	Cavalry	G. T. R.	Grand Trunk Railway
Co.	Company	Inf.	Infantry
Col.	Colonel	Lib.	Library
C.O.	Commanding Officer	Lieut.	Lieutenant
Cpl.	Corporal	Lt. Col.	Lieutenant Colonel
Ens.	Ensign	Sgt.	Sergeant
Esq.	Esquire	Vols.	Volunteers

Pay lists

Fenian Raid - 1866

Paris Detachment #1 Company, Paris Company[308]

Anderson, A.
Baird, Lieut. Andrew H.
Barker, Bilton
Bradwin, Edmund
Brown, David
Campbell, Joe
Carroll, Timothy
Church, Maitland
Conbrough, M.
Craig, Thomas
Davidson, Thomas
Elliot, Thomas
Evans, Thos.
Gouinlock, Robert W.
Hewson, Alexander
Hewson, William
Inksater, George
Isbister, Adam
Johnston, Wm.
Kay, John
Kinment, John
Laurence, Frank
Lee, George
Lee, Samuel
Lindsay, Alex
Lyons, John
Martin, John
McCummin, Thomas
McElroy, James
McKie, Samuel
McRae, John
Patten, Edw. Jr.
Patterson, Thos.
Patton, William
Puckridge, Charles
Revell, Abel
Reynolds, Elish
Rispin, John
Robinson, John
Rutherford, George
Scott, Walter
Simpson, Geo.
Skelly, Dennis
Spence, William
Springstead, Bartlett
Starr, Samuel
Starr, William
Stevenson, John
Sullivan, John
Symonds, Harry C.
Tinling, John
Tompkins, Fred
Torrance, John
Totten, Osborne
Warnock, James
Wass, John
White, William
Whitlaw, Clerk John M.
Wright, James

#1 Brantford Company, Fenian Raid March 8-31, 1866[309]

Ashton, Joseph
Atkinson, John
Batty, John
Bennes, William
Bond, Arthur
Boyd, J.
Boyd, William
Brown, Thomas
Cain, John
Cain, Thomas
Callis, Edward
Callis, Sgt. J.
Cawley, Henry
Clark, Cpl. Joseph
Copeland, Robert
Costello, Charles
Craig, Joseph
Crooks, H. P. S.
Dickie, Albert
Dickie, Arthur
Dickie, Capt. Hiram
Dimmock, George
Elliott, John
Foster, Jacob
Gray, John
Grenny, Francis J.
Hall, Walter
Harrison, Henry
Harrison, Sgt. Thomas
Heatley, Robert
Hildred, William
Hobson, Henry
Hoyt, Isaac
Kelly, Brock
Kennedy, Cpl. Wm.
Kerr, Robert
Kerr, William
McAlister, Henry
McGill, John
Montgomery, John
Nixon, S.
Page, James
Peirce, William Jr.
Pickering, Joseph
Sanders, T.
Sanders, William
Simms, Bugler Walter
Smith, Sgt. John
Smithson, John
Stubbs, William
Tanton, John
Thomas, Charles
Thomas, William
Totten, Warren
Transom, Thomas
Vaughan, James
Wallace, Edward
Wallace, Richard
Welsh, Robt.
Westrop, Cpl. R.
Wilkie, John
Willson, Robert

#2 Brantford Highland Company, Fenian Raid March 8-31, 1866[310]

Agnew, David
Batson, George P.
Bechtel, John
Blyth, Thomas
Clark, Alexander
Coyle, William
Cron, Archibald
Danskin, James
Doherty, John
Edwards, Michael
Ferguson, Robert
Gibson, Alexander
Gibson, John
Gibson, William
Gidden, William
Good, John
Gordon, Thomas
Grant, Capt. William
Grierson, James
Hawley, Edwin
Hext, James
Hunt, Albert
Hunter, Nathaniel
Ingleby, William
Inglis, Lieut. Joseph J.
Ivens, Thomas
Jamieson, Robert
Johnston, Thomas
Latham, P. J.
Mart, William
McCauley, Philip
McHaffie, Colour Sgt. John
McIntosh, P.
McIntyre, Angus
Mills, Edgar
Mitchell, David J.
Mitchell, William
Nicol, Lance Sgt. William
Scott, Thomas O.
O'Neil, Bugler John F.
O'Neil, James
Pattison, Ward
Peirce, John W.
Poole, Henry
Purves, Peter
Read, Henry W.
Read, Joseph
Read, Moses
Renwick, Thomas
Robson, Henry
Rountree, John
Roy, William F. T
Russell, Robert
Safford, Hiram
Spence, Ensign David
Stewart, Alexander
Sturgis, Albert
Sturgis, George
Truesdale, Thomas
Vogt, Sigmund
Wade, B. J.
Wallace, Robert
Watson, John
Watt, Robert
Williams, George
Willson, Cpl. Robert
Wood, Moras
Wright, James

Mount Pleasant Infantry Company, Fenian Raid March 8-31, 1866[311]

Anderson, Joseph
Anderson, Robert
Ashbaugh, George A.
Beam, Zenus
Blackburn, George
Brazier, Henry
Bryce, John
Buckman, William
Bye, George
Cleaver, Edward
Cleaver, William
Eadie, Robert
Folger, William
Forrest, Charles
Forrest, William
Frazie, James
Gallic, Sgt. David
Green, Thomas
Haren, Hilton
Hartley, Joseph
Heaton, Lieut. Crosley
Langyhar, William
Liscombe, John
Lund, Sgt. John
Malcolm, Finlay
Marten, Henry
McLaren, Cpl. John
McLenan, Edward
Phelps, E.
Raw, Sgt. John
Rodgers, William
Rutherford, David
Ryan, Charles
Ryan, William
Smith, Frances Allen
Smith, George W.
Smith, Walter
Thomas, David
Vanderlip, Edward
Vivian, William
Warfield, William H.

Paris Detachment #4 Company was the Drumbo Company, Fenian Raid, 1866[312]

Adams, A.
Adams, H.
Adams, Thos.
Batty, Henry
Boles, J. C.
Boughton, G.
Burgess, James
Cockburn, John
Coltart, Robt.
Cunliffe, A.
Dawson, Schuyler
Dier, David
Ellis, Frederick
Ellis, Hiram
Fair, Edward
Fisher, Cpl. Alex
Fricht, J. W.
Ghel, Fred
Graham, William
Hamilton, Charles
Henderson, Thomas
Holmes, Samuel
Howell, Capt. Wesley
Laidlaw, Lieut. John
Layden, Patrick
Lennon, John
Lorimer, Napoleon
Maynard, David
More, George
Patten, Ensign Ellmore
Prentice, David
Prentice, Joseph
Robinson, M.
Schofield, A.
Scott, Edward
Scott, James
Shaw, Daniel
Smith, J.
Stevenson, Wm.
Thurlby, Joseph
Watters, John J.
Watters, John
Whittrick, William

Pay list of the Paris Rifle Company, October 1856[313]

Abraham, Johnston
Abraham, Thomas
Allchin, Tho.
Allchin, William
Alma, Ensign William
Angus, George
Barclay, Sgt. Robert
Batty, C.
Cooper, Tho.
Craigie, David
Crosbie, Andrew
Crosbie, William
Dick, Alexander
Inksater, George
Jackman, Aaron
Kay, John
Lamb, D. M
Lamb, J.
Loutit, James
Macartney, George
Macartney, F. C.
Maxwell, G.
McLean, Alex
McSherry, Andrew
Miller, James
Mitchell, Geo.
Patton, William
Patton, S.
Pearce, F.
Phillipps, H.
Race, Henry
Ravill, W.
Remo, Wm.
Rickert, T.
Shannon, John
Sharpe, John Brereton
Smith, Benj.
Stanton, William
Stevenson, John

Dick, John
Edmunds, Crookshank
Finlayson, James
Fisher, Jas.
Gay, Andrew W.
Gray, Thos.
Havill, Phillip
Hearchner, Bugler John
Monighan, P.
Morton, Robert
Munro, Sgt. J.
Newman, John
Nimmo, James
O'Donnell, Cpl. Hugh
Patient, J.
Patton, A.
Stewart, Erskine
Sutherland, Henry
Sutherland, John
Tinling, R.
Webb, Drill Inst. Sgt. Wm.
Wheelihan, John
Young, A.
Young, Geo. M.

Pay list of the Paris Rifle Company May 1857[314]

Abraham, Johnston
Abraham, Thomas
Allchin, William
Alma, Ensign William
Baird, Hugh
Boughton, Levi
Buckley, Patrick
Buckley, Timothy
Cheeseboro, B.
Clode, George
Clode, Henry
Craigie, David
Crosbie, Andrew
Crosbie, William
Delill, Lewis
Dick, Alexander
Dick, John
Edmunds, Crookshank
Ellison, Matthew
Finlayson, James
Fisher, Jas.
Fitzgerald, John
Gay, Andrew W.
Havill, Philip
Inksater, George
Irwin, Jno.
Kay, John
Kirberger, A.
Loutit, James
Macartney, George
McElroy, James
McIvor, Angus
McLean, Alex
Miller, James A.C.
Mitchell, Charles
Morton, John
Morton, Robert
Munro, Sgt. J.
Newman, H.
Nimmo, James
Nowell, John
Oliver, Henry
Oliver, Thomas
O'Donnell, Hugh
Patience, J.
Patton, William
Preis, Wm.
Race, Henry
Remo, Wm.
Sharpe, John Brereton
Stanton, William
Stevenson, John
Stewart, Erskine
Sutherland, Henry
Sutherland, John
Tarrant, C.
Tinling, R.
Totten, Henry
Totten, Norman
Tougher, Hugh
Warnock, James
Webb, Drill Inst Sgt. Wm.
Young, Geo. M.

Pay list of the Paris Rifle Company April 1858[315]

Abraham, Johnston
Abraham, Thomas
Allchin, William
Alma, Ensign William
Baird, Hugh
Bell, A.C.
Boughton, Levi
Buckley, Patrick
Buckley, Timothy
Carter, George
Cheeseboro, B.
Clode, George
Craigie, David
Crosbie, Andrew
Crosbie, William
Delill, Lewis
Dick, Alexander
Dick, John
Hewson, Alexander
Hewson, William
Inksater, George
Irwin, Jno.
King, John
Kirberger, A.
Lee, Samuel
Loutit, James
Macartney, George
McCracken, A.
McElroy, James
McIver, Angus
McLean, Alex.
McSherry, Andrew
Miller, James
Mitchell, Charles
Morton, John
Morton, Robert
Oliver, Henry
Oliver, Thomas
Patton, William
Patton, S.
Phillips, E.
Price, W.
Remo, Wm.
Hubbard, Sgt. Robert
Scott, James
Sharpe, John Brereton
Stevenson, John
Stewart, Erskine
Sutherland, Henry
Sutherland, John
Tarrant, C.
Tinling, R.
Totten, Norman
Tougher, Hugh

Finlayson, James
Fisher, Jas.
Gay, Andrew W.
Munro, Sgt. J.
Newel, John
Nimmo, James Jnr.
Warnock, James
Watt, John

Pay list of the Paris Rifle Company December 1859[316]

Abraham, Johnston
Abraham, Thomas
Bell, A.C.
Boughton, Levi
Buckley, Patrick
Buckley, Timothy
Burgy, Adam
Carter, George
Clode, George
Copley, Robert
Craigie, David
Crosbie, Andrew
Crosbie, William
Dick, Alexander
Dick, John
Elligan, Michael
Finlayson, James
Hart, W. S
Hewson, Alexander
Hewson, William
Hubbard, Sgt. Robert
Inksater, George
Irwin, Jno.
King, John
Lee, Samuel
Loutit, James
McCrackin, A. J.
McDonald, John
McElroy, James
Miller, M.
Mitchell, Charles
Morton, John
Munro, Colour Sgt. J.C.
Nowell, John
Oliver, Henry
Oliver, Thomas
Patton, S.
Philips, Manuel
Pollock, Samuel
Remo, Wm.
Scott, James
Sharpe, Frederick
Sharpe, John Brereton
Sinan, J. C.
Spears, T.
Stevenson, John
Stewart, Erskine
Sutherland, John
Sutherland, Henry
Thompson, Wm.
Totten, Norman
Walter, William
Warnock, James

Pay list of the Paris Rifle Company November 1860[317]

Abraham, Johnston
Abraham, Thomas
Baker, J. A.
Bridle, Patrick
Buckley, Patrick
Burgy, Adam
Clarke, James
Clode, George
Conklin, Thomas
Copley, Robert
Crosbie, Andrew
Crosbie, William
Dick, Alexander
Finlayson, John
Frost, John
Hewson, Alexander
Hewson, William
Howell, John
Hubbard, Sgt. Robert
Hudson, William
Inksater, George
Irwin, Jno.
Jackman, Aaron
Lee, Samuel
Loutit, James
McElroy, James
Miller, M.
Mitchell, Charles
Munro, Sgt. J.
Oliver, Thomas
O'Neal, John
Patton, S.
Perkins, Wm.
Ryckman, Cornelius
Scott, James
Shannon, Robert
Sharpe, Frederick
Sharpe, John Brereton
Sinan, J. C.
Spence, William
Stewart, Erskine
Stewart, Robert
Sutherland, Henry
Totten, Norman
Wagner, Benjamin
Walton, William
Warnock, James

Pay list of the Paris Rifle Company November 1861[318]

Abraham, Johnston
Abraham, Thomas
Baker, J. A.
Bridle, Patrick
Burgy, Adam
Clarke, James
Hudson, William
Inksater, George
Irwin, Jno.
Lee, George
Lee, Samuel
Loutit, James
Patton, S.
Ryckman, Cornelius
Shannon, Robert
Sharpe, Frederick
Sharpe, John Brereton
Sinan, J. C.

Conklin, Thomas
Crosby, William
Davidson, Thomas
Dick, Alexander
Finlayson, John
Hawkins, Joseph F.
Hewson, Alexander
Hewson, William
Houghton, John
Hubbard, Sgt. Robert
McCummin, Thomas
McCummin, William
McElroy, James
McMurray, Ens. Wm.
Miller, M.
Morton, Robert
Munro, Sgt. J.
Nowell, John
Patton, William
Spence, William
Stewart, Erskine
Stewart, Robert
Sutherland, Henry
Torrance, John
Wagner, Benjamin
Walker, Robert
Walton, William
Warnock, James

Pay list of the Paris Rifle Company December 1862[319]

Capt. Wm. Patton (absent in England),

Abraham, Johnston
Abraham, Thomas
Bowman, M.
Bradwin, Joseph
Bridle, Patrick
Bullock, Joseph
Conklin, Thomas
Connell, Adam
Copley, Robert
Craig, Thomas
Davidson, Thomas
Finlayson, John
Haining, James
Hamilton, James
Hart, Henry
Hawkins, Joseph L.
Hewson, Alexander
Hewson, William
Houghton, John
Hubbard, Sgt. Robert
Inksater, George
Isbister, Adam
Kay, John
Lee, George
McCummin, Thomas
McCummin, William
McElroy, James
McMurray, Ens. Wm.
Morton, Robert
Nimmo, James
Patton, William
Ravell, F.
Rutherford, Ths.
Ryckman, Cornelius
Skelley, D.
Stewart, Erskine
Sutherland, Henry
Thomas, Henry
Torrance, John
Walker, Robert
Walton, William
Warnock, James
Watt, Surgeon John

Pay list of the Paris Rifle Company December 1864[320]

Anderson, A.
Baird, Lieut. Andrew H.
Barker, Bilton
Bradwin, Joseph
Bullock, Joseph
Capron, B.
Conklin, E.
Craig, Thomas
Crane, Henry
Ferguson, Robert
Haining, James
Hewson, Alexander
Hewson, William
Hubbard, Sgt. Robert
Inksater, George
Isbister, Adam
Kay, John
Lee, George
Lee, Samuel
Lindsay, Alex.
Markey, M.
Martin, E.
McCummin, Thomas
McElroy, James
McNaught, J. C.
Morton, John
Murphy, J.
Overell, Charles
Patton, Edward
Ravele, Jessie
Rispin, John
Robertson, J. M.
Shannon, Robert
Sharpe, Frederick
Smith, J.
Star, George
Star, William
Stevenson, John
Stewart, Erskine
Sutherland, Henry
Teskey, Wm.
Tinling, John
Torrance, John
Totten, Osborne
Walsh, Wm.
Walton, William
Warnock, James
Wass, John
Wright, James

Pay list of the Paris Rifle Company December 1865[321]

Anderson, A.
Angus, George
Baird, Lieut. Andrew H.
Barker, Bilton
Bradwin, Joseph
Brown, David S.
Conklin, E.G.
Craig, Thos.
Davidson, Thomas
Ferguson, R.
Haining, Jas.
Hewson, Alexander
Hewson, Corporal William
Inksater, George
Isbister, Adam
Kay, John
Lee, George
Lee, Samuel
Lindsay, Alexander
Lyons, John
Martin, John
McCummin, Thomas
McElroy, James
McKie, Samuel
Murphy, J.
Patton, Edward
Skelly, Dennis
Starr, George
Starr, Samuel
Starr, Wm.
Stevenson, John
Stewart, Erskine
Sullivan, Wm.
Tinling, John
Torrance, John
Totten, Osborne
Wall, Robt.
Walsh, Wm.
Warnock, James
Wass, John
Wright, James

Pay list of the 1st Brantford Rifle Company December 1864[322]

Ashton, J.
Atkinson, John
Aulsebrook, George
Aulsebrook, Thomas
Barker, Sgt. J.
Black, J.
Boyd, J.
Callis, Cpl. John
Callis, Edward
Carson,
Cawley, Henry
Chisholm, H.
Clark, Joseph
Clifford, J.
Craig, J.
Curry, W.
Drake, Sgt. William
Foster, Jacob
Gee, W.
Goodson, A.
Grantham, George
Grenny, Francis
Harrison, Sgt. Thomas
Hildred, William
Hoyt, Isaac
Kelly, Brock
Kennedy, Wm.
Kerr, Robert
Kerr, William
Lovett, C.
Lovett, Thomas
McAlister, A.
McAlister, John
McAlister, Henry
Montgomery, John
Nixon, S.
Pickering, Joseph
Pierce, William
Pilsworth, J.
Roberts, Samuel
Sanderson, J.
Shenahen,
Tanton, John
Thomas, Charles
Thomas, William
Vansickle, E.
Vaughan, James
Vogt, Bugler Sigmund
Watkins, E.
Watts, Alfred
Wells, J.
Westrop, Cpl. R.
White, D.
White, J.

Pay list of the 1st Brantford Rifle Company December 1865[323]

Ashton, Joseph
Atkinson, John
Battie, John
Black, J.
Boyd, J.
Callis, Edward
Callis, Sgt. J.
Cawley, Henry
Clark, Cpl. Joseph
Harrison, Sgt. Thomas
Hildred, William
Hoyt, Isaac
Kelly, Brock
Kennedy, Cpl. Wm.
Kerr, Robert
Kerr, William
McAlister, Henry
McAlister, John
Pickering, Joseph
Renney, W.
Richardson, A.
Sanders, J.
Smith, S.
Stubbs, William
Tanton, John
Thomas, Charles
Thomas, William

Clifford, J.
Craig, Joseph
Curry, W.
Drake, W.
Grenny, Francis
Montgomery, John
Nixon, C.
Page, James
Peirce, William
Vaughan, James
Watts, Alfred
Westrop, Cpl. R.
Witty, Bugler H.

Pay list of the 1st Brantford Rifle Company January 1866[324]

Ashton, Joseph
Atkinson, John
Batty, John
Bond, Arthur
Boyd, J.
Boyd, William
Brown, Thomas
Callis, Edward
Callis, Sgt. J.
Cawley, Henry
Clark, Cpl. Joseph
Clifford, J.
Copeland, Robert
Craig, Joseph
Crooks, H. P. S.
Dickie, Arthur
Dimmock, George
Elliott, John
Fransom, Tho.
Gray, John
Grenny, Francis
Harrison, Henry
Harrison, Sgt. Thomas.
Heatley, Robert
Hildred, William
Hobson, Henry
Hoyt, Isaac
Kelly, Brock
Kennedy, Cpl. Wm.
Kerr, Robert
Kerr, William
McAlister, Henry
McAlister, John
McGill, John
Montgomery, John
Nixon, S.
Page, James
Peirce, William
Pickering, Joseph
Rogers, H.
Sanders, T.
Sanders, William
Sears, J.
Smith, Sgt. John
Stubbs, William
Tanton, John
Thomas, Charles
Thomas, William
Vaughan, James
Wallace, Edward
Wallace, J.
Wallace, Richard
Watson, A.
Watts, Alfred
Welsh, Robt.
Westrop, Cpl. R.
Wilkie, John
Willson, Robert
Witty, Bugler H.

Pay list of the 2nd Brantford Highland Rifle Company 1864[325]

Agnew, David
Blacker, John
Blacker, Robert
Blyth, Thomas
Butters, Alexander
Coyle, William
Cron, Archibald
Danskin, James
Doherty, John
Foulds, John
Gibson, Alexander
Gordon, Thomas
Grierson, James
Griffin, F. M
Hammond, J. H.
Hawley, Edwin
Humbusch, Henry
Hunter, Nathaniel
Hutchinson, Alexander
Jamieson, Robert
Mart, William
McArthur, David
McCauley, Philip
McGibbon, Sgt. Daniel
McHaffie, Colour Sgt. John
McIntyre, Angus
Nesbit, John
Nichol, James F.
Nichol, William
O'Neil, Bugler John F.
Pattison, Ward
Pike, George
Poole, Henry
Read, Henry W.
Read, Joseph
Read, Moses
Renwick, Thomas
Robson, Henry
Rowe, John
Russell, Robert
Scott, Thomas O.
Smith, Wm.
Spence, Sgt. David
Spencer, James
Stewart, Alexander
Truesdale, Thomas
Walker, Charles
Watt, Robert
Willson, Robert
Wright, James

Pay list of the 2nd Brantford Highland Rifle Company 1865[326]

Agnew, David
Blacker, John
Blacker, Robert
Blyth, Thomas
Clark, Alexander
Coyle, William
Cron, Archibald
Danskin, James
Doherty, John
Foulds, John
Gibson, Alexander
Gibson, William
Gidden, William
Good, John
Gordon, Thomas
Grierson, James
Griffin, F. M
Hammond, J. H.
Humbusch, Henry
Hunter, Nathaniel
Ingleby, William
Jamieson, Robert
Mart, William
McCauley, Philip
McHaffie, Colour Sgt. John
McIntyre, Angus
Nesbit, John
Nicol, Cpl. William
Nicol, Jas. F.
O'Neil, Bugler John F.
Pattison, Ward
Pike, George
Poole, Henry
Read, Henry W.
Read, Joseph
Read, Moses
Renwick, Thomas
Robson, Henry
Russell, Robert
Scott, Thomas O.
Stewart, Alexander
Truesdale, Thomas
Wade, B. J.
Walker, Charles
Wallace, Robert
Watt, Robt.
Willson, Cpl. Robert

Pay list of the 2nd Brantford Highland Rifle Company June 1866[327]

Agnew, David
Batson, George P.
Bechtel, John
Blyth, Cpl. Thomas
Clark, Alexander
Coyle, William
Cron, Archibald
Danskin, James
Doherty, John
Ferguson, Robert
Gibson, Alexander
Gibson, John
Gibson, William
Gidden, Samuel
Gidden, William
Good, John
Gordon, Thomas
Grierson, James
Hawley, Edwin
Hext, James
Hunt, Albert
Ingleby, William
Jamieson, Robert
Johnston, Thomas
Latham, P. J.
Mart, William
McCauley, Philip
McHaffie, Colour Sgt. John
McIntosh, P.
McIntyre, Angus
Mitchell, David J.
Nicol, Cpl. William
O'Neil, Bugler John F.
O'Neil, James
Pattison, Ward
Peirce, John W.
Poole, Henry
Read, Henry W.
Read, Moses
Renwick, Thomas
Robson, Henry
Russell, Robert
Scott, Thomas O.
Sturgis, Albert
Sturgis, George
Truesdale, Thomas
Vogt, Sigmund
Wade, B. J.
Wallace, Robert
Watt, Robert
Williams, George
Willson, Cpl. Robert
Wright, James

Pay list of the Mount Pleasant Infantry Company 1864[328]

Anderson, Joseph
Anderson, William
Bryce, John
Buckman, William
Clark, Cpl. James
Decater, William
Eadie, Robert
Fear, Samuel
Franklin, William
Gallic, Sgt. David
Hartley, Joseph
Hartley, Robert
Lund, Sgt. John
Malcolm, Finlay
McLaren, Cpl. John
McLenan, Edward
Phelps, E.
Racey, Thomas
Raw, Sgt. John
Rutherford, David
Ryan, Charles
Smith, Frances Allen
Smith, Walter
Townsend, Elmer
Vanderlip, Edward
Vivian, William

Pay list of the Mount Pleasant Infantry Company September 1865[329]

Anderson, Joseph
Anderson, William
Baldwin, James R.
Beam, Zenus
Blackburn, George
Bryce, John
Buckman, William
Clark, Cpl. James
Cooke, Jno. Masson
Decater, William
Eadie, Robert
Fear, Samuel
Forrest, Charles
Forrest, William
Franklin, William
Gallic, Sgt. David
Hartley, Joseph
Hartley, Robert
Hawley, Gustavus E.
Knox, Robert
Liscombe, John
Longyhe, William
Lund, Sgt. John
McLenan, Edward
Malcolm, Finlay
McLaren, Cpl. John
Phelps, E.
Racey, Thomas
Raw, Sgt. John
Rutherford, David
Ryan, Charles
Ryan, William
Smith, Frances Allen
Smith, Walter
Swazie, Ralph
Townsend, Elmer
Vivian, William

Pay list of the Mount Pleasant Infantry Company May 1866[330]

Anderson, Joseph
Anderson, Robert
Anderson, William
Beam, Zenus
Blackburn, George
Brazier, Henry
Bryce, John
Buckman, William
Bye, George
Cleaver, Edward
Cleaver, William
Eadie, Robert
Fear, Samuel
Forrest, Charles
Forrest, William
Franklin, William
Gallic, Sgt. David
Green, Thomas
Hartley, Joseph
Hartley, Robert
Haren, Hilton
Languar, William
Liscombe, John
Lund, Sgt. John
Malcolm, Finlay
McLaren, Cpl. John
McLenan, Edward
Phelps, E.
Racey, Thomas
Raw, Sgt. John
Rodgers, William
Rutherford, David
Ryan, Charles
Ryan, William
Smith, Frances Allen
Smith, Walter
Thomas, David
Vanderlip, Edward
Vivian, William
Warfield, William H.

Pay list of the Drumbo Infantry Company January 1864[331]

Adams, A.
Adams, Thos.
Alkins, J.
Bailey, C.
Brown, S. D.
Burgess, I. L.
Burgess, John
Burgess, Francis
Clark, G. W.
Clark, Henry
Clasz, S.
Fricht, J. W.
Hamilton, Charles
Harrison, Geo.
Henderson, Thomas
Howell, C.
Hubbart, Cpl. Albert
Hughson, George
Lennon, John
Lockhart, William
Martin, F. S.
McCaffey, Thos.
Peck, Almon
Phillips, E.
Pinkham, William
Prentice, Joseph
Rounds, J. B.
Schermerhorn, F.
Shaw, Daniel
Smith, J.
Smith, Robert
Staples, John
Stevenson, Wm.

Crandell, Reuben
Dier, David
Fritch, W. Allen
Pasmore, Thomas
Pattulo, William
Thurlby, Joseph
Whittrick, William

Pay list of the Drumbo Infantry Company 1865[332]

Adams, A.
Adams, Thos.
Auld, Allen
Blackstock, J.
Brown, S. D.
Clark, Henry
Cockburn, John
Crawford, J.
Ellis, Hiram
Fair, Edward
Fisher, Cpl. A.
Fricht, J. W.
Graham, William
Grant, Geo.
Hamilton, Charles
Henderson, Thomas
Howell, C.
Kenny, Cpl. L. B.
Lennon, John
Lockhart, William
Martin, Cleodel
Martin, Cpl. Jesse
Maynard, David
McCaffey, Thos.
Patterson, Francis
Pattulo, William
Peck, Almon
Pinkham, William
Prentice, David
Prentice, Joseph
Shaw, Daniel
Smith, J.
Stephenson, Sgt. Wm.
Stevenson, James
Thurlby, Joseph
Thurlby, Thos.
Vroon, Cpl. A.
Watters, John
Watters, John J.
Whittrick, William

Pay list of the Drumbo Infantry Company April 1866[333]

Adams, A.
Adams, H.
Adams, Thos.
Bailey, C.
Bawtinhmer, C.
Blackstock, J.
Brown, S. D.
Burgess, James
Cockburn, John
Cunliffe, A.
Ellis, Hiram
Fair, Edward
Fisher, Cpl. A.
Fricht, J. W.
Graham, William
Hamilton, Charles
Henderson, Thomas
Hill, Alex
Howell, Capt. Wesley
Kenney, L. B.
Laidlaw, Lieut. John
Lennon, John
Lockhart, William
Maynard, David
McCain, John
McKenzie, C.
Patton, Ensign F. E.
Pattulo, William
Peck, Almon
Pinkham, William
Prentice, David
Prentice, Joseph
Robinson, M.
Schofield, A.
Scott, James
Shaw, Daniel
Smith, J.
Stevenson, J.
Stevenson, Wm.
Thurlby, Joseph
Thurlby, Thos.
Watters, John
Watters, John J.
Whittrick, William

Rules For Home Guards [334]

It being thought desirable that precautions should be taken to provide for the maintenance of order in the event of lawless aggression, the undersigned Officers and Men of the _______ Battalion_______ County Militia, tender their services as a Home Guard for that purpose. All the undersigned are alike willing to bear arms in defense of their homes and families, but are not all equally able to devote any considerable portion of their time to the acquisition of a Military training. The Guard will therefore be divided into two classes, viz., the "Active" and the "Reserve" Guards.

I.—To the Members of the "Reserve" Guard, directions as to their conduct, should an alarm be raised, will be given, and the stations to which they will in that event repair, will be pointed out to them, but no service will, under other circumstances, be required of them.

II.—Any person desirous of becoming a Member of the Guard shall signify the same to the Officer in command, and on receiving his approval, shall subscribe his name to these Rules.

III.—The members of the Active Guard shall assemble at such time and place as the Officer in command may direct, for the purpose of drilling, at least once in each week.

IV.—The Officer commanding the Guard shall keep a correct list of the Members present and absent at each Drill, and make a return of the same to the Officer commanding the Battalion.

V.—Any Member of the Active Guard who shall, without leave from his Commanding Officer, absent himself from any Drill or Parade for four days in succession, unless such absence be caused by sickness or absence from his place of residence, shall be compelled to return to the Officer commanding, all arms, accoutrements, &c., the property of Her Majesty, that may have been entrusted to him.

VI.—Each Member of the Guard shall be personally responsible for any property of the Government that may be entrusted to him, which property shall be presented by him for inspection once in each month.

VII.—Any Member of the Guard receiving clothing, arms, or accoutrements, the property of the Government, will be held responsible for any damage the same may suffer, if caused by neglect while in his hands; and any Member attending drill or parade with his arms or accoutrements in a dirty state, or out of repair, shall be subject to reprimand, or to expulsion, at the discretion of the Commanding Officer.

Signatures of the Active Guard	Age	Residence	Signatures of the Reserve Guard	Age	Residence

Officers of the Paris Rifle Company

authorized by G. O. June 26, 1856 [335]

Major	Macartney, George	Nov. 20, 1856	
Captain:	Macartney, George	June 26, 1856	Appointed to the 100th Regiment
	Patton, William	May 20, 1858	promoted to Major, May 20, 1863
	Baird, Andrew. H.	Nov. 30, 1866	resigned retaining rank
Lieutenant:	Patton, William	June 26, 1856	
	Alma, Ensign William	May 20, 1858	left the district
	Morton, Robert	Apr. 28, 1859	left limits
	Baird, Lieut. Andrew H.	Dec. 1, 1865	
	Totten, Osborne	Nov. 30, 1866	
Ensign:	Alma, Ensign William	June 26, 1856	
	Morton, Robert	May 20, 1858	
	Allchin, William	Apr. 28, 1859	left limits Aug. 1860
	McMurray, Ens. Wm.	Aug. 8, 1860	left limits June 26, 1863
	Totten, Warren	June 26, 1863	transferred to 1st Brantford Vols.
	Totten, Osborne	May 19, 1865	
	Hewson, William	Nov. 30, 1866	
Surgeon:	Watt, John	Sept. 24, 1857	

Officers of the 1st Brantford Rifle Company

authorized by G. O. Dec. 13, 1861 [336]

Captain:	Alger, Major William N.	Dec. 13, 1861	
		Jan. 6, 1865 became paymaster Central Administrative Battalion	
	Dickie, Hiram	Jan. 6, 1865	
	Curtis, David	Nov. 30, 1866	
Lieutenant:	Hearnden, Robert	Dec. 13, 1861	left limits
	Williams, Frederick	Jan. 30, 1863	left limits
	Totten, Warren	Dec. 1, 1865	resigned Mar. 30, 1866
	Curtis, David	June 15, 1866	
	McAlister, Henry	Nov. 30, 1866	
Ensign:	Williams, Frederick	Dec. 13, 1861	
	Dickie, Hiram	Jan. 30, 1863	
	Totten, Warren	Jan. 13, 1865	
	McAlister, Henry	June 15, 1866	

Officers of the 2nd Brantford Highland Rifle Company

authorized by G. O. July 3, 1862 [337]

Captain:	Grant, William	July 3, 1862	38th Brant Paymaster Nov. 30, 1866
Lieutenant:	Inglis, Joseph J.	July 3, 1862	
Ensign:	Carr, Matthew X.	July 3, 1862	
	Spence, David	Dec. 2, 1864	

Officers of the 3rd Brantford Infantry Company

authorized by G. O. June 1, 1866 [338]

Captain:	Lemmon, Henry	June 1, 1866
Lieutenant:	Ballachey, John	June 1, 1866
Ensign:	Minore, John	June 1, 1866

Officers of the Mount Pleasant Infantry Company

authorized by G. O. Jan. 30, 1863 [339]

Captain:	Ellis, Allan Wallace	Jan. 30, 1863	resigned May 18, 1864
	Heaton, Crosley	May 25, 1866	
Lieutenant:	Phelps, Wm. E.	Jan. 30, 1863	resigned Oct. 2, 1863
	Heaton, Crosley	Oct. 2, 1863	
	Fear, Samuel Wilcox	May 25, 1866	
Ensign:	Eadie, Robert	Jan. 30, 1863	
	Fear, Samuel	Apr. 13, 1866	
	Rutherford, David	July 6, 1866	

Officers of the Burford Infantry Company

authorized by G. O. Aug. 17, 1866 [340]

Captain:	Wooden, Ira C.	Aug. 17, 1866	resigned Nov. 9. 1866
	Yeigh, Edmund	Nov. 9, 1866	resigned Jul. 16, 1869
Lieutenant:	Byrne, Claudius	Aug. 17, 1866	
Ensign:	Yeigh, Edmund	Aug. 17, 1866	

Officers of the Burford Cavalry Troop

authorized by G. O. Sept. 7, 1866 [341]

Captain:	Bingham, Jacob	Sept. 7, 1866
Lieutenant:	Marshall, William	Dec. 14, 1866
Cornet:	Lloyd-Jones, Tho.	Dec. 14, 1866

Officers of the Drumbo Infantry Company
authorized by G. O. Jan. 30, 1863 [342]

Captain:	Howell, Wesley	Jan. 30, 1863	retired retaining rank, Nov. 30, 1866
	Laidlaw, John	Nov 30, 1866	
Lieutenant:	Hill, R. T.	Jan. 30, 1863	resigned June 10, 1864
	Laidlaw, John	June 10, 1864	
	Patullo, George R.	Nov. 30, 1866	
Ensign:	Muma, Charles Andrew	Jan. 30, 1863	resigned June 10, 1864
	Rodgers, James	June 10, 1864	
	Waters, John	Nov. 30, 1866	left the limits Mar. 27, 1869

Officers of the Tuscarora Rifle Company
authorized by G. O. Dec. 11, 1862 [343]

Captain:	Kerr, William John Simcoe	Dec. 11, 1862
Lieutenant:	Clench, Henry	Dec. 11, 1862
Ensign:	Buck, John	Dec. 11, 1862

Officers of the Onondaga Infantry Company
authorized by G. O. Feb. 6, 1863 [344]

Captain:	Whiting, Matthew	Feb. 6, 1863
Lieutenant:	Waugh, John H.	Feb. 6, 1863
Ensign:	Herdsman, Richard	Feb. 6, 1863

Officers of the Grand Trunk Railroad Brigade, 1st Company, 5th Battalion
authorized by G. O. Apr. 27, 1866 [345]

Captain:	Patterson, Thomas	Apr. 27, 1866
Lieutenant:	Penfold, Henry Augustus	May 11, 1866
Ensign:	Barker, James	May 11, 1866

Officers of the Grand Trunk Railroad Brigade, 2nd Company, 5th Battalion
authorized by G. O. Apr. 27, 1866 [346]

Captain:	Gilbert, Charles	Apr. 27, 1866
Lieutenant:	Lund, Frederick	May 11, 1866
Ensign:	Clifford, Gowan	May 11, 1866

Officers of the Grand Trunk Railroad Brigade, 3rd Company, 5th Battalion
authorized by G. O. Apr. 27, 1866 [347]

Captain:	Larmour, Robert	Apr. 27, 1866
Lieutenant:	McLean, William	May 11, 1866
Ensign:	Savage, Alfred	May 11, 1866

Fenian Raid Medals

In 1899 the services of the veterans of the Fenian invasion were recognized by Queen Victoria with the striking of a Canadian General Service Medal.

The obverse bore the effigy of Queen Victoria. On the reverse was the Canadian ensign within a wreath of maple leaves and the word 'Canada' at the top.

After comparing the Fenian raid pay lists of the Brant companies with the official records, it would appear that not all men applied for the medal. In the case of the 1866 veterans it would have been 33 years after the call to service.

The following information comes from the official records in the National Archives of Canada.

Figure 48 Canadian General Service Medal, Fenian Raid

Men Awarded the General Service Medal, Fenian Raid - 1866

Paris Volunteer Rifle Company [348]

NAME	NATURE OF SERVICE
Baird, Lieut. & Capt. Andrew H.	On active service 8th Mar 1866 to 30th June 1866 at Paris.
Barker, Bilton	Fenian raid. On active service 8th March 1866 to June 16th 1866 at Paris. Expecting to go to the front. Guard mounting Grand Trunk Railway bridge.
Bradwin, Edmund Wm.	Fenian raid 1866. 1st June 1866 to July 1866 at Paris Ontario - attack expected.
Carroll, Timothy	Fenian raid 1866. Guarding Grand Trunk Railway bridge on active service 8th March to 2nd June 1866 at Paris. Expected to go to Ridgeway in June. Guard mounting was duty specially assigned.
Davidson, Thomas G.	8th March to 31st March 1866 at Paris.
Elliott, Thomas	8th March to June 1866 at Paris.
Evans, Thomas	Fenian raid 1866. Daily drill, expecting marching orders to go to Fort Erie. On active service Mar. 1866 at Paris. Battalion and company drill in constant expectation of marching orders.
Gouinlock, Robert Wallace	Fenian raid 1866. Guarding railway and bridge 8th to 31st March, 2nd to 16th June, and two weeks in September at Thorold - expecting attack.
Hewson, Alexander	Fenian raid. Expecting to go to the front. On active service 8th March 1866 to 10th June 1866 at Paris guarding Grand Trunk Railway bridge.
Hubbard, Sgt.-Major Robert	Fenian raid. Guard mounting.. On active service 6th March 1866 to June 23rd, 1866 at Paris. Repel Fenian raiders under arms, drilling, guarding Grand Trunk Railway bridge. Expecting to go to the front.
Johnson, William	from spring to fall of 1866 at Niagara district.
Kay, John	Fenian raid. Guarding railway bridge. On active service 8th March to 10th June 1866 at Paris.
Kay, Sgt. David A.	Always ready for service March to June 1866 at Paris.
Laurence, Frank F.	Guard mounting, drilling, etc. 6th March 1866 to 23rd June 1866 at Paris. Expected to go to the front any day.
Lee, Corporal Samuel	Fenian raid 1866. Repelling Fenian raid on active service March 1866 to June 1866 at Paris - mounting guard on Grand Trunk Railway bridge.
Lyons, John R.	March to June 1866 Paris.
McCammon, Cpl. Thomas	Fenian raid. On active service 8th March to 16th June, 1866 at Paris. Guard mounting and other services required by order.
McElroy, Sgt. James	March to June 1866 at Paris and September.
McKie, Samuel	8th March 1866 to 16th June 1866 at Paris, special duty drilling, guarding Grand Trunk Railway bridge - church parades etc.
McRae, John	8th to 31st March 1866 at Paris.
Puckridge, Chas.	Spring to Fall 1866 in Niagara District.
Robinson, Thomas	On active service March 1866 to June 1st 1866 at Paris. Guard mounting Grand Trunk Railway bridge
Robinson, John	Guarding Grand Trunk Railway bridge March and June 1866 at Paris. Expecting orders to go to the front daily.
Rutherford, George	Fenian raid.. On active service March 8th 1866 to June 13th 1866 at Paris. Guard mounting, drill every day, church parade and Grand Trunk Railway bridge.
Simpson, George T.	Fenian raid. On active service March 1866 to June 1866 at Paris. Guard Grand Trunk Railway bridge.
Spence, William	1st June to 1st July 1866 at Paris. Was in the reserve and with a Co. that was on guard.
Springstead, Bartlett	27th March to June 1866 at Paris.
Stevenson, John	Fenian raid 1866. Guard mounting and guarding Grand Trunk Railway bridge

Paris Volunteer Rifle Company [348]

NAME	NATURE OF SERVICE
	8th March 1866 to 16th June 1866 at Paris. Expected to be ordered to the front.
Symonds, Harry Charles	Mar 1866 to disbandment in June 1866 at Paris about 3 weeks - attack expected.
Torrance, John	Fenian raid. Guarding Grand Trunk Railway bridge. On active service 8th Mar 1866 to 22nd June 1866 at Paris. Expected to go to the front.
Totten, Osborne	Fenian raid 1866. 8th to 31st Mar 1866 and 2nd to 16th June 1866 at Paris guarding railway bridge and awaiting orders.
Warnock, James	Fenian raid. Guard mounting Grand Trunk Railway bridge. On active service 6th March 1866 to 13th June 1866 at Paris.
Wass, John	June to October 1866 at Paris and Thorold.
Whitlaw, John M.	8th March 1866 to 31st March 1866 at Paris also 2nd to 16th June 1866. Ordered to Ridgeway but countermanded.
Wright, James	Fenian raid. Guard mounting. On active service 6th March 1866 to 16th June 1866 at Paris. Expected to go to the front. Guarding Grand Trunk Railway bridge.
Wrigley, George	2nd June 1866 to about 3 weeks at Paris. Expecting to go to Niagara or elsewhere.

1st Brantford Volunteer Rifle Company [349]

NAME	NATURE OF SERVICE
Ashton, Joseph	8th March to 16th July 1866 at Brantford and Dunnville. Guarding prisoners in jail at Toronto and guarding dam at Dunnville.
Atchinson, John	8th March to 16th July 1866 at Brantford and Dunnville. Guarding prisoners in jail at Toronto and guarding dam at Dunnville.
Batty, John Fitton	2nd to 18th June 1866 at Dunnville and Brantford. Attack expected and took place at Limeridge.
Bond, Arthur	8th March to 16th July 1866 at Brantford and Dunnville. Escorting prisoners to Toronto, guarding prisoners in jail at Toronto and guarding dam at Dunnville.
Boyd, William	8th March to 16th July 1866 at Brantford and Dunnville. Guarding prisoners in jail at Toronto and guarding dam at Dunnville.
Cain, Thomas	May to July 1866 at Brantford. Special duty at Dunnville, Thorold and Ridgeway.
Callis, Edward	June to August 1866 Port Colborne, Fort Erie, Dunnville, Brantford and Toronto.
Callis, Sgt. J.	8th March to 16th July 1866 at Brantford and Dunnville. Guarding prisoners in jail and escorting them to Toronto and on guard at Dunnville.
Craig, Joseph	8th March to 16th July 1866 at Brantford and Dunnville. Guarding prisoners in jail and escorting them to Toronto and on guard at Dunnville.
Crooks, H. P. S.	8th March to 16th July 1866 at Brantford and Dunnville. Guarding prisoners in jail and guarding dam at Dunnville.
Denton, Edward J.	1st June to Sept. 1866. Guard duty at Dunnville.
Dickie, Albert Alex	8th March to 16th July 1866 at Brantford and Dunnville. Guarding prisoners in jail and escorting them to Toronto and guarding dam at Dunnville.
Dickie, Arthur Wellington	8th March to 20th July 1866 at Dunnville on the dam that supported the Welland canal.
Dickie, Captain Hiram	8th March to 16th July 1866 at Brantford and Dunnville. Guarding prisoners at Brantford and guarding feeder Welland Canal at Dunnville.
Foster, Jacob	8th March to 16th July 1866 at Brantford and Dunnville. Guarding prisoners at Brantford and dam at Dunnville.
Gray, John	8th March to 16th July 1866 at Brantford and Dunnville. Guard duty at

1st Brantford Volunteer Rifle Company [349]

NAME	NATURE OF SERVICE
	Brantford taking prisoners to Toronto jail.
Grenny, Col.-Sgt. Francis Jas.	Mar. 8th to July 1866 at Brantford in charge of prisoners.
Hall, Walter	8th March to 16th July 1866 at Brantford and Dunnville. Guarding prisoners at Brantford and dam at Dunnville.
Harrison, Sgt. Thomas	8th March to 16th July 1866 at Brantford. Guard duty in Brantford and taking prisoners to Toronto jail.
Heatley, Robert	8th March to 16th July 1866 at Brantford. Guarding prisoners in Brantford jail and escorting them to Toronto.
Hildred, Wm.	8th March to 16th July 1866 at Brantford and Dunnville guarding prisoners in Brantford and conveying them to Toronto.
Kelly, Brock Green	8th March to 16th July 1866 at Brantford and Dunnville. Guarding prisoners in Brantford and conveying them to Toronto.
Kerr, Wm. N.	8th March to 16th July 1866 at Brantford and Dunnville. Guarding prisoners in Brantford jail escorting them to Toronto and guard duty at Dunnville.
Knox, Wm. Robert	March 8th to July 16th at Brantford and Dunnville guarding supplies etc.
McAlister, Lieut. Henry	8th March to 16th July 1866 at Brantford and Dunnville. June 2nd prisoners in Brantford jail and taking them to Toronto June 9th and guard duty at Dunnville to 16th July 1866.
McGill, John James	8th March to 16th July 1866 at Brantford and Dunnville. Guarding prisoners in Brantford jail and taking them to Toronto and guard duty at Dunnville.
Miller, Henry L.	July 1st to 16th 1866 at Dunnville garrison duty.
Montgomery, John	8th March to 16th July 1866 at Brantford and Dunnville. Guarding prisoners in Brantford and escorting them to Toronto.
Nixon, S.	8th March to 16th July 1866 at Brantford and Dunnville. Taking prisoners to Toronto and guard duty at Dunnville.
Peirce, William	8th March to 16th July 1866 at Brantford and Dunnville. Guarding prisoners at Brantford and dam at Dunnville.
Pickering, Joseph	8th March to 16th July 1866 at Brantford and Dunnville. 2nd June guarding Fenian prisoners in Brantford 9th June taking them to Toronto and on guard at Dunnville 16th July.
Sanders, T.	8th March to 16th July 1866 at Brantford and Dunnville 2nd June guarding prisoners in Brantford. 9th June taking them to Toronto and on guard at Dunnville 16 July.
Sanders, William	8th March to 16th July 1866 at Brantford and Dunnville. Guarding prisoners at Brantford 9th June taking them to Toronto and guard duty at Dunnville 16th July.
Sears, Bugler James W.	8th March to 16th July 1866 at Brantford and Dunnville. Guarding prisoners in Brantford and taking them to Toronto 9th June and guard duty at Dunnville 16th July 1866.
Sims, Walter	8th March to 16th July 1866 at Brantford and Dunnville. Guarding prisoners at Brantford and dam at Dunnville.
Smith, Arthur W.	Garrison duty waiting orders 8th March to 16th July 1866 at Brantford and Dunnville. Guard duty and taking prisoners to Toronto and special duty at Dunnville.
Tanton, John	8th March to 16th July 1866 at Brantford and Dunnville -guarding prisoners in Brantford and escorting them to Toronto and guarding dam at Dunnville.
Thomas, Charles	8th March to 16th July 1866 at Brantford and Dunnville guarding prisoners in Brantford and dam at Dunnville.
Thomas, Wm. James	May to July 1866 at Brantford. Special duty Dunnville, Thorold and

1st Brantford Volunteer Rifle Company [349]

NAME	NATURE OF SERVICE
	Ridgeway.
Vaughan, James	8th March to 16th July 1866 at Brantford and Dunnville. Guarding prisoners at Brantford escorting them to Toronto and guard duty at Dunnville.
Wallace, Edward	8th March to 16th July 1866 at Brantford guarding prisoners and escorting them to Toronto.
Wallace, Richard	8th March to 16th July 1866 at Brantford and Dunnville. Guarding prisoners and escorting them to Toronto and guarding dam at Dunnville.
Welsh, Robert	8th March to 16th July 1866 at Brantford and Dunnville. Taking prisoners to Toronto and barrack duty at Dunnville.
Westrop, Cpl. R.	8th March to 16th July 1866 at Brantford and Dunnville. Guarding prisoners and guard duty at Dunnville.

#2 Brantford Highland Rifle Company [350]

NAME	NATURE OF SERVICE
Agnew, David	Fenian Invasion 1866. Usual garrison duty, awaiting orders. From 8th Mar. 1866 to 16th June 1866 at Brantford. On June 2nd company took charge of 59 Fenian prisoners, guarded them in the jail here and escorted them to the old jail Toronto and delivered them to sheriff Jarvis on the 9th June 1866.
Bechtel, John	"
Blacke, Robert	"
Buck, Judson W.	"
Cron, Archibald	"
Danskin, Lance Cpl. James	"
Edwards, Michael	(Mar to Nov 1866 at Brantford)
Ferguson, Robert	(March & June 1866 at Brantford, guard duty)
Gibson, John	"
Gidden, Samuel	"
Gidden, William	"
Gordon, Thomas	"
Grant, Capt. William	"
Heyd, Charles B.	"
Ingleby, Wm.	"
Jamieson, Robert	"
Johnston, Thomas	(March 8th to June 16th , 1866 at Brantford, in charge of prisoners)
Latham, Bandmaster P. J.	"
Mart, William	"
McCauley, Philip	"
McIntosh, P.	"
Mitchell, David J.	"
Nicol, Lance Sgt. William	"
O'Neil, Bugler John	"
O'Neil, James	"
Pattison, John Ward	"
Peirce, John W.	"
Pike, George	"
Renwick, Thomas	"
Russell, Robert	"
Scott, Lance Cpl. Thomas O.	"

#2 Brantford Highland Rifle Company [350]

NAME	NATURE OF SERVICE
Spence, Ensign David	"
Sturgis, Albert	"
Truesdale, Thomas	"
Wade, B. J.	"
Watt, Robert	"
Willson, Cpl. Robert M.	"
Wood, Mario	"
Wright, James	"

Mount Pleasant Infantry Company [351]

NAME	NATURE OF SERVICE
Anderson, Robert	2nd to 22nd June 1866 at Paris. Special duty guarding Reserve base and internal line of communication.
Ashbaugh, Geo. Albert	2nd to 22nd June 1866 at Paris. Special duty guarding Reserve base and internal line of communication.
Blackburn, Geo. Albert	2nd to 22nd June 1866 at Paris. Special duty guarding Reserve base and internal line of communication.
Bryce, John	2nd to 22nd June 1866 at Paris. Special duty guarding Reserve base and internal line of communication.
Brazier, Henry	2nd to 22nd June 1866 at Paris. Special duty guarding Reserve base and internal line of communication.
Bye, George	June 2nd to 22nd 1866 at Mt. Pleasant and Paris guard duty.
Cleaver, Edward	7 March to June 1866 guarding bridge at Paris
Decator, William	2nd to 22nd June at Paris
Forest, Charles	2nd June to 15th July 1866 at Paris
Hartley, Cpl. Joseph	2nd to 22nd June 1866 at Paris. Special duty guarding Reserve base and internal line of communication.
Hartley, Robert	2nd to 22nd June 1866 at Paris. Special duty guarding Reserve base and internal line of communication.
Liscombe, John	2nd to 22nd June 1866 at Paris. Special duty guarding Reserve base and internal line of communication.
Lund, Sgt. John	1st to 21st June at Paris. Special duty guarding reserve base and interior line of communication.
Malcolm, Cpl. Finlay	2nd to 22nd June 1866 at Paris. Special duty guarding Reserve base and internal line of communication.
McLaren, Cpl. John W.	2nd to 22nd June 1866 at Paris. Special duty guarding Reserve base and internal line of communication.
Phelps, E. Lord	2nd to 22nd June 1866 at Paris. Special duty guarding Reserve base and internal line of communication.
Rutherford, David	May to latter part of June 1866 at Paris
Ryan, Charles	2nd to 22nd June 1866 at Paris. Special duty guarding Reserve base and internal line of communication.
Ryan, Wm.	2nd to 22nd June 1866 at Paris. Special duty guarding Reserve base and internal line of communication.
Smith, Cpl. Frances Allen	2nd to 22nd June 1866 at Paris. Special duty guarding Reserve base and internal line of communication.
Steward, William	2nd to 22nd June at Paris
Thomas, David Henry	2nd to 22nd June 1866 at Paris. Special duty guarding Reserve base and internal line of communication.
Vivian, Cpl. William	2nd to 22nd June at Paris

Mount Pleasant Infantry Company [351]

NAME	NATURE OF SERVICE
Warfield, Bugler William H.	June 1st to July 15th , 1866 at Paris.
Westbrook, Henry Shaver	2nd to 22nd June 1866 at Paris. Special duty guarding Reserve base and internal line of communication.

Drumbo Volunteer Infantry Company [352]

NAME	NATURE OF SERVICE
Howell, Capt. Wesley	Fenian raid 1866. March 8th to 18th June 1866. On the 8th March 1866 I was ordered by the D. A. G. to muster my company for active service. On 9th left H.Q. Drumbo for Woodstock left there for Paris on the 10th; remained there about 3 weeks doing garrison and other duty under Maj. Patton; returned to H.Q. Drumbo remaining under orders. On June 1 we were again ordered away to join London and Oxford Vol. Companies under Major McPherson at Paris then proceeded to Port Colborne, Ridgeway, Fort Erie then returned to London - disbanded about 18th June 1866.
Adams, A.	Fenian raid 1866. March 8th to May 1866. Drumbo, Woodstock, Paris - was sick in June but in August 1866 was with my company at Thorold under Col. Richardson.
Adams, H. B.	Fenian raid March 8th to 18th June 1866
Adams, Thomas	"
Cockburn, John	"
Cunliffe, Alexander	"
Fair, Cpl. Edward	"
Fricht, J. W.	"
Howes, John	"
Kinney, Sgt. Lewis B.	"
Layden, Patrick	March to April 1866 at Paris.
Lockhart, Colour Sgt. William	Fenian raid March 8th to 18th June 1866
Lorimer, Napoleon	"
Maynard, Sgt. David C.	"
Peck, Almon	"
Pinkham, William	"
Prentice, David	"
Prentice, Joseph	"
Prentice, Wm.	"
Slaght, Philip	Mar 8 to June 18, 1866 at Paris, Ridgeway, Port Colborne, Fort Erie and London.
Smith, J.	March to April 1866
Watters, John J.	Fenian raid March 8th to 18th June 1866
Whittrick, William	"

Articles and Regulations of the 1st Volunteer Rifle Company of Brantford [353]

Article 1 Government - This company, in all that relates to its organization, discipline and duty shall be governed according to the Militia Law of the Province, and by such orders as may from time to time, be issued by the Commander in Chief.

Article 2 Uniform - The uniform shall consist of Rifle Green Tunics, single breasted, with scarlet facings and black and shoulder strap; collar and cuffs slightly braided.

Rifle Green trousers with stripes of black braid on a scarlet stripe down the legs.

Article 3 Arms and Accoutrements

Section 1- The arms and accoutrements shall be those furnished by the Provincial government, subject to the provisions of Section 21 of the abstracts from the Militia Law appended to these Articles and Regulations.

Section 2 - The arms, accoutrements and knapsacks (and the overcoats during the season they are not required for use) shall be delivered into the custody of the armourer.

Article 4 Admission of Members

Section 1 - All applications for membership shall be made personally to the Commanding Officer and the Candidate shall be proposed by Members who are able to state his name, residence and occupation. The claim of the Recruit will there upon (unless known to the presiding Officer) be submitted to the Board herein mentioned, and on the next drill or business meeting of the company, the decision shall be made known, which if unfavourable shall reject him; if admitted, his name shall be enrolled at once in the Register of the Company.

Section 2 - Any person applying to be admitted as a member of the Company, shall not be under 5 feet 5 inches in height, and shall with his application hand to the Treasurer the sum of fifty cents towards the clothing fund, which shall be returned to him in the event of his rejection by the Company.

Article 5 Duty of Members

Section 1 - It shall be the duty of each member to attend all regularly appointed drills of the Company, and all Public parades properly uniformed, armed and accoutred, when called on to do so by the Commanding Officer, unless satisfactory reasons can be assigned.

Section 2 - It shall be the duty of the non-commissioned officers and privates, to preserve their arms and accoutrements in proper order and to deposit them in the Armoury immediately after drill or parade.

Section 3 - Each officer shall pay to the treasurer the sum of twenty-five cents and each non-commissioned officer and private the sum of ten cents at each monthly meeting to defray current expenses.

Section 4 - The Colour Sergeant shall keep the roll, which he shall call at the opening of every meeting, and a statement of absentees and delinquents shall be by him handed over to the Board of Management for consideration. He shall divide the Company into three squads, each under the charge of a Sergeant and Corporal. It shall be their duty to serve all notices or orders that may emanate from the Commanding Officer or Board of Management; in the absence of the Colour Sergeant the Senior Sergeant present shall assume his duties.

Section 5 - Each Sergeant shall provide himself with a copy of the Muster Roll.

Article 6 Board of Management

Section 1 - The Board of Management shall consist of a Secretary, a Treasurer, and five members; the Officers and Colour Sergeant being (ex officio) Members of the Board.

Section 2 - At all business meetings the Captain shall preside, in his absence the Lieutenant shall take the chair, and in the absence of both the Ensign. Three members and one officer shall form a quorum. No business transacted at such meetings shall be valid unless presided over by one of the Officers.

Section 3 - The Secretary shall keep correct minutes of all proceedings at meetings of the Company or Board of Management and shall conduct the correspondence.

Section 4 - The Treasurer shall collect all monies due to, and pay all amounts due by the Company as authorized by the Board; he shall of necessity open an account in one of the Banks of the Town, in which all monies received shall be deposited in the name of the Company, and his cheques countersigned by the Commanding Officer shall be valid in all cases; he shall have the privilege of keeping twenty dollars in hand to meet current expenses.

Section 5 - It shall be the duty of the Board to examine all accounts against the company, and authorize payment when approved of; to inspect the Treasurer's books, and statements of receipts and expenditures previous to the annual meeting and to prepare a report of the same; to make arrangements for the purchase of any necessities for the Company with the sanction of the Captain; to investigate charges made against any member , if preferred by three or more members of the Company, and to report on the same, also to inquire into the character of persons desirous of joining the Company who may be unknown to the officers.

Article 7 Meetings

Section 1 - The Annual meeting of the Company shall be held on the third Wednesday in January in each year, when the election of the Board of Management shall take place. A business meeting shall be held on the third Wednesday of every month.

Section 2 - There shall be a day held once a week if possible, to commence punctually at half past seven o'clock P.M. at which the Muster roll shall be called.

Section 3 - At all business meetings one officer, one non-commissioned officer and ten privates shall form a quorum.

Section 4 - A special meeting of the Company may be called at any time, by order of the Commanding Officer.

Article 8 Fines and Penalties

Section 1 - Any member absenting himself from a Monthly, or a special meeting of the company, without furnishing a sufficient case, shall be fined ten cents; the Board of Management shall have the power of deciding upon the validity of the excuse offered.

Section 2 - Any member who shall without good cause, or permission granted by the Commanding Officer absent himself from any of the six days drill, a special or public parade, shall pay for each days absent a fine of twenty-five cents.

Section 3 - No member shall be allowed to bear his arms or accoutrements except when on duty or by consent of the officers, or to lend any portion thereof to any person not a member of the company under a penalty of fifty cents.

Section 4 - Any member showing insubordination or being intoxicated at drill or parade or acting in any manner calculated to bring disgrace upon himself or the Company shall be subject to dismissal at the discretion of the officers.

Section 5 - No member shall be entitled to vote who is more than three months in arrears of subscription or who has not paid all fines legally due by him to the Company.

Section 6 - The willful infraction of any of these Articles and Regulations, for which no special rule is made on three separate occasions proved before the Board of Management, shall subject the party offending to expulsion from the Company at the option of the Officers.

Section 7 - Any member wishing to leave for any space of time shall have the privilege of obtaining a written furlough from the Captain for three months, during which time he shall be exempt from all fines and penalties for non-attendance.

Section 8 - No member shall leave the Company without first giving two months notice in writing to the Commanding Officer (except when he may be expelled) when all his interest in the funds shall cease.

Article 9 Honourary Members

Any person may become an Honourary member of the Company by paying the sum of Four dollars to the Treasurer, he shall be entitled to drill on any of the ordinary drill nights of the Company.

No.

Province of Ontario

Location Certificate

Under 1 Edward VII Cap. 6.

This is to Certify

that Samuel Giddens

having served as a Private in The Brantford Rifles

in Ontario in 1866 on the occasion of The Fenian Raid

is hereby authorized to enter upon and occupy The North Half

of Lot Number Nine in the Fifth concession

of the Township of Ratter containing 160 acres

under and subject to the provisions of said Act.

Given under my hand at Toronto

this Twenty-Third day of September A.D. 1903

Countersigned

Figure 49 Location Certificate authorizing land grant to Fenian Raid veterans.

Militia Acts, General Orders and Memoranda

Militia Act of 1855 [354]

XXI. The Active Militia of the Province in time of peace, shall consist of Volunteer Troops of Cavalry, field Batteries, foot Companies of Artillery, and Companies of Infantry armed as Riflemen, to be formed at places to be designated by the Commander in Chief, but not exceeding in the whole sixteen Troops of Cavalry, seven field Batteries of Artillery, five foot Companies of Artillery, and fifty Companies of Riflemen: the total of such Volunteer Corps not exceeding five thousand Officers and Men.

XXII. Each Volunteer Troop of Cavalry, Company of Foot Artillery, or Company of Riflemen, shall consist of a Captain, a Lieutenant, a Cornet, Second Lieutenant or Ensign, three Serjeants, three Corporals, a Trumpeter or Bugler, and not exceeding forty-three Privates, except in Companies of Riflemen wherein the number of Privates may be any number from forty-three to seventy-five; and each Field Battery of Artillery shall consist of a Captain, two first Lieutenants, a Second Lieutenant, a Serjeant Major, three Serjeants, three Corporals, three Bombardiers, a Trumpeter, a Farrier, fifty-nine Gunners and Drivers, including Wheelers, Collar maker and Shoeing-smith, fifty-six horses, exclusive of Officers' horses, and of four spare horses when the Battery is called into actual service.

XXXII. The Volunteer Militia Companies shall be drilled and exercised, at such time in each year and at such places as the Commander in Chief may from time to time appoint; the Volunteer Field Batteries being so drilled and exercised during twenty days in each year, of which twenty days ten shall be continuous, and the other Volunteer Corps once in each year during ten continuous days, (Sundays not reckoned in either case,) and the Companies under drill being encamped during the whole or any part of the period for drill, if the Commander in Chief shall see fit.

XXXIV. For each day on which they shall be so drilled, the officers and men of the said Volunteer Companies shall be paid by the Province the following sums:

Captains per diem	,0	10	6
Lieutenants	0	7	6
Second Lieut., Cornets or Ensigns	0	6	6
Non-Commissioned Officers and Privates	0	5	0

and a further sum of five shillings per diem for each horse actually and necessarily present and used for such drill, whether belonging to officers or to privates.

XXXVIII. The said Volunteer Companies shall be liable to be called out in aid of the ordinary Civil power in case of riot or other emergency requiring such services, and shall when so employed receive from the Municipality in which their services shall be required, the rates of pay above mentioned, and a further sum of two shillings and six pence per man per diem for additional expenses, and shall be also provided with proper lodging by such Municipality...

XL. The Officers, non-Commissioned Officers and men of Volunteer Companies, shall, while they shall continue such, be exempt from serving as Jurors or Constables; and whenever they shall have served as such in one or more Volunteer Companies during a term of seven years, such exemption shall continue after the expiration of said term.

XLV. No person shall be an Officer of Militia unless he be one of her Majesty's subjects by birth or naturalization, and shall have taken the oath of allegiance.

LI. All contraventions of this Act and of Regulations or Orders lawfully made or given under it, when the Militia or that portion thereof to which the offender belongs, is not called out for actual service, shall be punishable by penalties to be imposed by one or more Justices of the Peace and in a summary manner as hereinafter provided, and Courts Martial shall not be held.

LV. When the Militia of any local division are called out, in case of war, insurrection or invasion, or imminent danger thereof, all Companies of Volunteers in such division, shall be included in the order and shall obey the Officer issuing it.

LXV. The Militiamen so taken or drafted for actual service from the Sedentary Militia, shall serve during one year unless sooner disbanded, and may then be replaced by others taken as aforesaid, and shall not be liable to be again taken until all others in the same class shall have been taken; but the men in Volunteer Militia Companies shall serve for the time for which they have engaged to serve, which time shall not be less than five years, subject, however, to be determined on one month's notice as hereinbefore mentioned. Provided that no Volunteer shall leave the service, either with or without notice, at any time when the Militia are called out, unless he be regularly discharged or have served out the time for which he engaged.

LXVII. The Militia so called out and every Officer or man belonging to it, from the time he shall be ordered, taken or drafted for actual service, shall be subject to the Articles of war and to the Act for punishing Mutiny and desertion and all other Laws...

XC. Any Officer, non-commissioned Officer or Militiaman, who shall disobey any lawful order of his superior officer, or shall be guilty of any insolent or disorderly behaviour towards such Officer, shall thereby incur a penalty of one pound five shillings, for each offence.

XCIV. Any Officer or Man of a Volunteer Militia Company who, when such Company shall be lawfully called upon to act in aid of the Civil power, shall refuse or neglect to go out with such Company, or to obey any lawful order of his Superior Officer or of any Magistrate, shall thereby incur a penalty of five pounds for each offence.

XCVI. Any person lawfully required under this Act to furnish any carriage, horse or ox, for the conveyance or use of any Troops or Militia, who shall neglect or refuse to furnish the same, shall thereby incur a penalty of two pounds for each such offence.

Militia Act of 1859 [355]

15. The Commander in Chief shall have full power to constitute any number of Rifle Companies of the Active Militia at any one locality or within any one district, not being less than six or more than ten Companies into a Regiment or Battalion, and to assign or appoint thereto by commission, a Lieutenant-Colonel, two Majors, one Adjutant, one Pay-Master, one Quarter-Master, one Surgeon and one Assistant Surgeon whose rank and authority therein shall be the same as in the relative positions in Her Majesty's service, and such Regiment or Battalion shall be subject, in so far as the same are not inconsistent with the provisions of the Militia Laws of this Province, to the Queen's Regulations for the Army published by authority; and any such Lieutenant-Colonel shall have the authority to appoint Staff Sergeants for any Battalion.

General Orders and Memoranda [356]

HEADQUARTERS,

Toronto, 6th December 1855

No. 2

Officers appointed to the Active Militia Force of the Province, and who have previously held commissions in the Militia, will take rank according to the dates of such former Commissions when serving with other Corps, and not from the date of their appointments to the Active Force; and Officers thus situated will send in a Return of the dates of their former Commissions and Corps they belonged to, to the Adjutant General.

DE ROTTENBURG,
Adj. Genl. Militia

Daily Pay of Officers in Her Majesty's Service, 1856 [357]

REGIMENTAL RANK	Cavalry			Artillery			Infantry		
	£	s	d	£	s	d	£	s	d
Lieutenant-Colonel, "in Sterling money"	1	3	0	0	18	1	0	17	0
Major	0	19	3	0	16	9	0	16	0
Captain	0	14	7	0	12	1	0	11	7
Captain, with higher rank by Brevet	--	--	--	0	13	1	0	13	7
Lieutenant	0	9	0	0	6	10	0	6	6
Cornet, 2nd Lieutenant or Ensign	0	8	0	0	5	7	0	5	3
Pay-Master, on appointment	0	12	6	0	12	6	0	12	6
Adjutant	0	10	0	*0	8	6	†0	3	6
Quarter-Master, on appointment	0	8	6	0	7	10	0	6	6
Surgeon	0	15	0	0	15	0	0	15	0
Assistant Surgeon	0	10	0	0	10	0	0	10	0
Veterinary Surgeon	0	8	0	--	--	--	--	--	--

* If 2nd Captain, 12s. 9d. H In addition to the pay as a Subaltern.

ADJUTANT GENERAL'S OFFICE
Toronto, 15th February, 1859.

(Circular Memorandum)

As most of the Cavalry Corps of the Active Force are scattered all over the County in which they are serving, and as it appears they have several places of *rendez-vous* for "Sword Exercise," His Excellency the Commander in Chief desires the Officer Commanding the several Troops to use their discretion in carrying out the General Order No 1, of the 4th inst., as far as the "Swords" are concerned, but it must be distinctly understood that the Pistols are to be kept in Store, except in cases when the Corps may be called out in aid of the Civil Power.

By Command,
D. MACDONELL and
A. DE SALABERRY,
Deputy Adjutant Genls. Militia.
U. & L. C.[358]

HEADQUARTERS,
Quebec, 17th May, 1861

Militia General Order, No. 1 [359]

ACTIVE FORCE

His Excellency the Commander in Chief being of opinion that the Officers commanding corps of the Volunteer Force should have some progressive promotion in the Militia of the Province for long service and for the efficiency of their corps, has been pleased to establish the following regulations for this purpose, viz.:

1st. That all Captains commanding corps of the Active Force, who have served as such continuously since the year 1856, inclusive and whose corps are at present efficient in every respect to the satisfaction of the Inspecting Officer, shall be promoted to the rank of Major in the Militia.

2nd. That henceforth, (except in special cases,) the rank of Major shall be granted after five years actual service as Captain of a corps which is fully uniformed and efficient in every respect to the satisfaction of the Inspecting Officer.

3rd. That henceforth, (except in special cases,) promotion to the rank of Lieutenant Colonel in the Militia will be granted only to Officers who have served five years consecutively as Majors at the head of one or more corps who are fully uniformed and efficient in every respect to the satisfaction of the Inspecting Officer,---thus requiring ten years to attain the rank of Lieutenant Colonel from the period of the first appointment as Captain.

Militia General Order, No. 3, August 30, 1861 [360]

Directs that all Rules and Regulations adopted by Corps of Volunteers under the provisions of the Militia Law, must be signed by every Member of the Corps previous to being sent to Head Quarters for approval.

Extract from the Volunteer Militia Act [361]

24. Any Corps of Volunteers may make, agree upon and enter into, such articles, rules and regulations for the discipline and good management of the same as they may think proper, to be sanctioned by the Officer Commanding such Corps and to be by him transmitted for the approval of the Commander-in-Chief; and any such articles, rules and regulations, in so far as they are not inconsistent with this Act, shall, when so approved, but not before, be enforced, and the penalties which may be thereby imposed shall, whenever they are incurred, be recoverable in the manner mentioned in any of the sections of *An Act respecting the Militia* incorporated with this Act, by the Officer designated for that purpose in such rules and regulations, to such uses as may be therein directed.

HEADQUARTERS,
Quebec, 20th December, 1861

Militia General Order, No. 2 [362]

His Excellency the Commander in Chief has had under his consideration the obvious disadvantages which must exist in the event of any Militia corps being dressed in uniforms differently from any of those worn by Her Majesty's regular Troops with whom they may be required to act.

His Excellency therefore has ordered the re-publication of the Circular Letter from the office of the Adjutant General of Militia, of the 19th May, 1860, by which the uniform of the Active Militia Force is prescribed, in accordance with the Militia Law; and His Excellency strongly urges the attention of Officers in command of corps of the Active Force to the necessity of a strict compliance with such General Order; and in respect to such corps as may have provided themselves with Undress

Uniform of Grey Cloth, His Excellency urges that the Regulation Uniform should be procured by them soon as their circumstances will permit.

[Copy]

"Circular,
Active Force. *ADJUTANT GENERAL'S OFFICE*
Quebec, 19th May, 1860,

Sir,---In accordance with section 31 of the Consolidated Militia Laws, His Excellency the Commander in Chief has been pleased to prescribe the following pattern for all clothing ***to be furnished in future*** *by the Volunteer Force of the Province; viz.*

Field Batteries and Foot Companies of Artillery
Blue Tunics and Trowsers, the same as the Royal Artillery

Cavalry
Blue Tunics, single breasted, with Scarlet facings and white cord - Officers to wear Silver Lace
Blue Trowsers with white stripes down the legs

Rifle Corps or Companies
Rifle Green Tunics, single breasted, with Scarlet facings and Black Cord Shoulder Strap; collar and cuffs slightly braided.
Rifle Green Trowsers with two stripes of Black Braid on a scarlet stripe down the legs: the Highland Companies are recommended to wear Tunics, or Jackets, and Trews the same as those used in the regular service, the material and facings of the Tunic or Jacket to be in uniform with the other Rifle Corps.
The Buttons of the Tunics of each Arm of the Force to be of the same description as those worn in the regular service, encircled with the words, "Volunteer Militia Canada.'

Head Dress
His Excellency is pleased to leave the description of the future Head Dress to be decided by the Force themselves: but, with a view to uniformity at each Station, it must be so arranged that each Arm of the Service will always appear on Parade with the same style of Head Dress---the Highland Companies however will continue to wear such Head Dress as may be considered most suitable to themselves.
In thus prescribing a Uniform for the Force, His Excellency earnestly desires to impress upon the Commanding Officers and all others concerned, the expediency of keeping the expense of the uniform of the Volunteer Corps as low as possible---His Excellency is satisfied that the most simple uniform will be the most serviceable, and that the several Corps will be maintained in a more efficient state by diminishing the cost of the soldier's outfit."

D. MACDONELL, Lieut. Colonel,
A. DE SALABERRY, Lieut. Colonel,
Depy. Adjt Genls. of Militia,
U. & L. C.

Militia General Order No. 1, November 6, 1863 [363]

Notifies that no person can be appointed a Field Officer of Volunteers until he has given proof before a Board of Examiners of his competence to command a Battalion at Battalion Drill in the field, and has obtained a Certificate to that effect from such Board.

HEADQUARTERS,

Quebec, 11th May, 1864

General Order

With reference to Section 35 of the Volunteer Militia Act, His Excellency the Commander-in-Chief is pleased to direct as follows, with regard to promotions and appointments in the Volunteer Force:

1st. Officers may receive provisional promotions in the Volunteer Force.

2nd. Gentlemen not now holding commissions may be provisionally appointed as Company Officers in the Volunteer Force.

3rd. Such promotions and appointments shall be confirmed substantively only on condition that the persons provisionally nominated shall, within twelve months from the date of the provisional promotion or appointment, comply with such conditions with respect to examinations as may be laid down in any future General Order.

A. DE SALABERRY, Lieut. Colonel,
WALKER POWELL, Lieut. Colonel,
Depy. Adjt Genls. of Militia,
L. & U. C. [364]

Weapons

The principal weapon used by the early volunteer militia prior to 1866 was the .577 calibre Enfield rifle in a long and short version. The long rifle was issued to the rank and file and the short version to the company sergeants.[365] The long rifle shown below had characteristic three groove rifling, three clamping bands adjusted with a screw, slotted and knurled ramrod, adjustable rear sight graduated to 800 yards, plain blade sight mounted on a square sight block which also served as the locking blade for the bayonet.

There were other weapons in use by the militia during this time period. During the 1866 Fenian invasion several thousand Peabody and Spencer carbines were bought from the U. S. government and used. [366] One company of the Queen's Own Rifles carried Spencer carbines at the battle of Ridgeway.[367] But the Enfield and the Snider-Enfield were the standard issue weapons of the time.

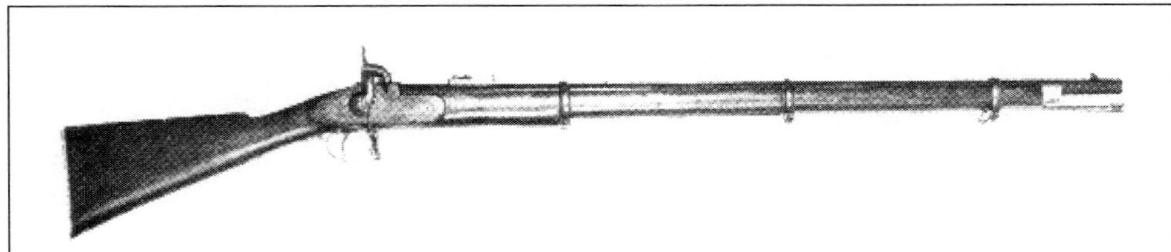

Figure 50 Pattern 1858 Enfield Long Rifle. Calibre .577 Barrel length 39 inches. This was the most widely used rifle in the Canadian Militia until the introduction of the Snider-Enfield in 1867.

Uniforms

Circular Memo Sept. 5, 1864: [368]

Informs Officers of the Militia that the following Articles may be obtained from the Militia Department at the prices stated.

Infantry	
Blue Frock,	$13.50
Each pair of Silver Stars or Crowns,	1.50
Scarlet Tunic,	22.00
Each pair of Gold Stars or Crowns,	1.50
Trowsers, Oxford Mixture,	6.00
Shako, with Ornaments and Silk Glazed Cover,	4.00
Sword, with Leather Scabbard, Gilt Mountings, and Chamois-lined Bag,	11.00
Sword, with Steel Scabbard, Gilt Mountings, and Chamois-lined Bag,	11.00
White Patent Leather Sword Belt, with Plate "Canada Militia,"	4.50
Gold Sword Knot	2.40
Silk Sash, weighing 8 ozs.,	7.80
Silk Sash, weighing 10 ozs.,	9.50
Forage Cap,	2.40
Badge for Forage Cap,	1.75
Infantry Serjeant's Sashes	1.75
Rifles	
Tunic,	20.00
Each pair of Silk Stars or Crowns,	1.00
Trowsers, Oxford Mixture,	6.00
Shako, with Ornaments and Silk Glazed Cover,	3.25
Sword, with Chamois-lined Bag,	8.50
Black Patent Sword Belt,	2.40
Black Leather Sword Knot,	0.50
Black Patent Shoulder Belt and Pouch, with Ornaments,	5.10
Forage Cap,	2.40
Badge for Forage Cap,	1.00

Artillery	
Sword with Lined Bag,	8.50
White Patent Sword Belt,	4.50

Officers making a requisition for any of the above articles, will be required to send with the requisition a deposit receipt from the Bank of Montreal, to the credit of the Receiver General of the Province, for such sum as will cover the price of the articles required; and in all cases where Shakos, Tunics and Trowsers are required, it will be necessary to give the size of the Head, the Height, and the Waist and Breast measure.	
Clothing	
Great Coat,	4.00
Tunic, Artillery,	5.50
Tunic, Infantry,	5.25
Tunic, Rifles,	5.50
Trowsers, Artillery per pair,	4.25
Trowsers, Infantry per pair,	2.00
Busbies for Artillery,	2.70
Shakos for Infantry and Rifles,	1.37
Chevrons for Serjeants and Corporals,	0.122
Military School Clothing	
Scarlet Serge Tunic,	2.25
Serge Trowsers per pair,	2.00
Forage Cap,	0.50
Ornament for Forage Cap,	0.122
Fur Cap,	1.00

All monies recovered under the foregoing Clause of the Volunteer Militia Act will be deposited in the Bank of Montreal, and the deposit receipt therefor sent to this Department.

Circular Memo March 20, 1865: [369]

Publishes for the information of Officers Commanding Volunteer Corps and Military Schools, &c., &c., the following list of prices of Government Stores, &c., so that in case of loss or damage the same may be recovered under the provisions of the following clause of the Militia Act.

"44. If any person designedly makes away with, sells, pawns, wrongfully destroys, wrongfully damages, or negligently loses, any property or thing issued to him or in his possession as a Volunteer,---or wrongfully refuses or wrongfully neglects to deliver up, on demand, any property or thing issued to him or in his possession as a Volunteer,---the value thereof shall be recoverable from him, with costs, as a penalty under this Act is recoverable; and he shall also for every such offence of designedly making away with, selling, pawning, or wrongfully destroying as aforesaid, be liable, on the prosecution of the Commanding Officer of the Corps or Battalion, to a penalty not exceeding twenty dollars, nor less than five dollars with or without imprisonment for any term not exceeding six months."

Arms	$ 4	Small Stores	$ 4
Short Enfield Rifle complete,	21.16	Knapsack complete,	2.50
Sword Bayonet for Short Enfield Rifle,	1.82	Haversack,	0.33
Leather Scabbard for Short Enfield Rifle,	0.75	Bugle and Strings,	5.00
Long Enfield Rifle complete,	15.20	Nipple wrench with Cramp,	0.60
Bayonet for Long Enfield Rifle,	1.50	Nipple wrench without Cramp,	0.25
Leather Scabbard for Long Enfield Rifle,	0.32	Ball Drawer,	0.03
Accoutrements		Brass jag,	0.03
Pouch Belt, shoulder,	0.75	Spare Nipple	0.03
Waist Belt,	0.50	Snap Cap and Chain	0.03
Frogs for Waist Belt,	0.25	Muzzle stopper	0.03
Cap Pocket,	0.25	50 round Pouch,	1.50
Sling,	0.25	20 round Pouch,	1.00

Figure 51 Pre 1866 uniform. Note the Canadian Militia cap badge and reference to 'C. W.' an abbreviation for Canada West.

Figure 52 Uniform issued to soldiers of the 38th Brant Battalion of Infantry, after 1866. The numeral '38' was worn as a cap badge.

This section was researched and written by Lt. Col. Edward Pancoe, 56th Field Artillery Regt., R.C.A.(Ret.)

56TH FIELD ARTILLERY REGIMENT, ROYAL CANADIAN ARTILLERY ORGANIZATION, PERPETUATIONS AND BATTLE HONOURS

BRANT COUNTY

(Independent Companies)

The Volunteer Militia Rifle Company of Paris
26 Jun 1856
(GO 26 Jun 1856)

The 1st Volunteer Militia Rifle Company of Brantford
13 Dec 1861
(MGO 13 Dec 1861

Volunteer Militia Highland Rifle Company
(Brantford)
3 Jul 1862
(MGO 3 Jul 1862)

Mount Pleasant Infantry Company
30 Jan 1863
(MGO 30 Jan 1863)

Brantford Infantry Company
1 Jun 1866 (MGO 1 Jun 1866)

Burford Infantry Company
17 Aug 1866
(MGO 17 Aug 1866)

Newport Infantry Company
31 Aug 1866
(MGO 31 Aug 1866)

Drumbo Infantry Company
30 Jan 1863
(MGO 30 Jan 1863)
Incorporated as
No. 3 Company, 38th "Brant Battalion of Infantry"
30 Nov 186638th "Brant Battalion" of Infantry
28 Sep 1866
(MGO 28 Sep 1866)

Redesignated:
38th "Brant Battalion of Rifles"
24 Mar 1871
(MGO 18/1871)

Redesignated:
38th "Brant" Battalion or "Dufferin Rifles"
3 Jul 1874
(MGO 18/1874)

Redesignated:
38th Battalion "Dufferin Rifles of Canada"
28 Sep 1883
(MGO 21/1883)

Redesignated:
38th Regiment "Dufferin Rifles of Canada"
8 May 1900 (MO 105/1900)

HALDIMAND COUNTY

(Independent Companies)

The 1st Volunteer Militia Rifle Company of Dunnville
24 Jul 1856
(GO 24 Jul 1856)

York Volunteer Militia Rifle Company
27 Aug 1862
(MGO 27 Aug 1862)

Caledonia Volunteer Militia Rifle Company
27 Aug 1862
(MGO 27 Aug 1862)

Oneida Infantry Company
6 Jul 1866
(MGO 6 Jul 1862)

Walpole Infantry Company
31 Aug 1866
(MGO 31 Aug 1866)

Cheapside Infantry Company
14 Sep 1866
(MGO 14 Sep 1866)

37th "Haldimand Battalion of Rifles"
28 Sep 1866
(MGO 28 Sep 1866)

Redesignated:
37th Regiment "Haldimand Rifles"
3 May 1900
(MGO 105/1900)

Reorganized and redesignated:
The Haldimand Rifles
perpetuating
114th Battalion, C. E. F.
1 May 1920
(MGO 66/1920)
Disbanded and reorganized
1 Apr 1921
(MGO 84/1921)

Disbanded 14 Dec 1936.
Amalgamated with
The Dufferin Rifles of Canada and
"C" Company,
3rd Machine Gun Battalion,
C. M. G. C.
to form

⇓

NORFOLK COUNTY

(Independent Companies)

The 1st Volunteer Militia Rifle Company of the County
of Norfolk (Villa Nova)
15 Oct 1861
(MGO 15 Oct 1861)

Simcoe Volunteer Militia Rifle Company
22 Jan 1862
(MGO 22 Jan 1862)

Port Rowan Volunteer Militia Rifle Company
23 Jan 1863
(MGO 23 Jan 1863)

Walsingham Volunteer Militia Rifle Company
Jan 1863
(MGO 23 Jan 1863)

Waterford Infantry Company
17 Aug 1866
(MGO 17 Aug 1866)

Simcoe Infantry Company
17 Aug 1866
(MGO 17 Aug 1866)

39th "Norfolk Battalion of Rifles"
28 Sep 1866
(MGO 28 Sep 1866)

Redesignated
39th Regiment
"Norfolk Rifles"
8 May 1900
(MGO 105/1900)
Reorganized and redesignated:
The Norfolk Regiment
perpetuating
133rd Battalion, C. E. F.
1 May 1920,
(GO 66/1920)

Disbanded and reorganized
1 May 1921
(MGO 118/1921)

Redesignated:
The Norfolk Regiment of Canada
15 Nov 1928
(MGO 186/1928)

Disbanded 14 Dec 1936
Converted and redesignated:
25th (Norfolk) Field Brigade, RCA
15 Dec 1936
(GO 189/1936)
consisting of: 33rd Field Battery, 41st Field

56TH FIELD ARTILLERY REGIMENT, ROYAL CANADIAN ARTILLERY ORGANIZATION, PERPETUATIONS AND BATTLE HONOURS

BRANT COUNTY	HALDIMAND COUNTY	NORFOLK COUNTY
Reorganized and redesignated: The Dufferin Rifles of Canada perpetuating 4th, 36th, 125th and 215th Battalions, C. E. F. 1 May 1920 (GO 66/1920)	⇓	Battery, 42nd Field Battery, 46th Field Battery (How) authorized but held in abeyance 2 Feb 1920 (GO 13/1920)
Disbanded and reorganized 1 Sep 1920 (GO 66/1920)		Redesignated: Field Batteries, C.A. 1 Jul 1925 (GO 82/1925)
Disbanded 14 Dec 1936 Amalgamated with The Haldimand Rifles and "C" Company, 3rd Machine Gun Battalion, C. M. G. C. to form	⇓	Title "Royal" granted Canadian Artillery 3 Jun 1935 (GO 53/1935)
	⇓	41st and 42nd Field Batteries redesignated respectively 41st/ 46th and 33rd/ 42nd Field Batteries, R.C.A. 1 Aug 1942 (GO 353/1942)
⇓		Redesignated: 45th RESERVE** (Norfolk) Field Regiment, RCA 5 Sep 1942 (GO 352/1942)
⇓	⇓	41st/ 46th and 33rd/ 42nd Field Batteries redesignated respectively 41st and 42nd Medium Batteries, RCA and the Regiment redesignated: 25th Field Regiment (Norfolk Regiment) RCA 1 Apr 1946 (GOs 116, 161/1946)
⇓	⇓	46th Field Battery (How.) redesignated 46th Field Battery and re-allocated to 44th Field Regiment, RCA 1 Apr 1946 (GO 115/1946)
⇓	⇓	41st and 42nd Field Batteries converted to 41st and 42nd Medium Batteries, RCA. 33rd Field Battery re-crested and allocated to 8th Field Regiment, RCA 28 Nov 1946 (GO 289/1946)
⇓	⇓	
	⇓	

56TH FIELD ARTILLERY REGIMENT, ROYAL CANADIAN ARTILLERY ORGANIZATION, PERPETUATIONS AND BATTLE HONOURS

BRANT COUNTY / HALDIMAND COUNTY	NORFOLK COUNTY
The Dufferin and Haldimand Rifles of Canada 15 Dec 1936 (GO 29/1937)	** "RESERVE" incorporated into title in accordance with GO 273/1940. This indicated a unit of the Canadian Army which was not a part of the Active Service Force.
Converted and reorganized: 56th Light Anti-Aircraft Regiment (Dufferin and Haldimand Rifles), RCA consisting of HQ and the 54th, 69th and 169th Light Anti-Aircraft Batteries Royal Canadian Artillery 1 Apr 1946 (GO 115/1946).*	The Regiment and its two batteries amalgamated with 56th LAA Regt (Dufferin and Haldimand Rifles), RCA to form

56th Field Regiment (Dufferin and Haldimand Rifles), RCA,
54th, 69th and 169th Batteries, RCA,
1 Oct 1954 (CAO Supp Part "B" Issue No 412/1954)

56th Field Artillery Regiment (Dufferin and Haldimand Rifles)
13 Jun 1960 (CAO Supp Part "B" Issue No. 670/1960)
Amalgamated with the 57th Field Artillery Regiment (2nd & 10th Dragoons), RCA
10th, 171st and 172nd Field Artillery Batteries
to form

56th Field Artillery Regiment, RCA
10th, 54th and 69th
Field Artillery Batteries
1 Apr 1970

BATTLE HONOURS

The Dufferin Rifles of Canada, GO 110, 15 Sep 1929,
The Norfolk Regiment, GO 71, 15 May 1930,
The Haldimand Rifles, GO 71, 15 May 1930

PERPETUATIONS

4th, 36th, 114th, 125th, 133rd and 215th Battalions, C. E. F.
2nd Dragoons, 25th Brant Dragoons, 10th Brant Dragoons, 2/10 Dragoons

308. RG9 1C3, Vol. 16, 'Paris' file
309. RG9 1C3, Vol. 10, 'Brantford file'
310. RG9 1C3, Vol. 10, 'Brantford file'
311. RG9 1C3, Vol. 15, 'Mount Pleasant file'
312. RG9 1C3, Vol. 12, 'Drumbo file'
313. RG9 1C3, Vol. 16, 'Paris file'
314. RG9 1C3, Vol. 16, 'Paris file'
315 RG9 1C3, Vol. 16, 'Paris file'
316. RG9 1C3, Vol. 16, 'Paris file'
317. RG9 1C3, Vol. 16, 'Paris file'
318. RG9 1C3, Vol. 16, 'Paris file'
319. RG9 1C3, Vol. 16, 'Paris file'
320. RG9 1C3, Vol. 16, 'Paris file'
321. RG9 1C3, Vol. 16, 'Paris file'
322. RG9 1C3, Vol. 10, 'Brantford file'
323. RG9 1C3, Vol. 10, 'Brantford file'
324. RG9 1C3, Vol. 10, 'Brantford file'
325. RG9 1C3, Vol. 10, 'Brantford file'
326. RG9 1C3, Vol. 10, 'Brantford file'
327. RG9 1C3, Vol. 10, 'Brantford file'
328. RG9 1C3, Vol. 15, 'Mount Pleasant file'
329. RG9 1C3, Vol. 15, 'Mount Pleasant file'
330. RG9 1C3, Vol. 15, 'Mount Pleasant file'
331. RG9 1C3, Vol. 15, 'Drumbo file'
332. RG9 1C3, Vol. 12, 'Drumbo file'
333. RG9 1C3, Vol. 12, 'Drumbo file'
334. 31 Victoria, (S. P. No. 35), 1868, pg. 28 The Annual Report on the State of the Militia,
335. RG9 1C6 Vol. 18, pg 72, Vol. 19, pg 55, Vol. 20, pg 194
336. RG9 1C6 Vol. 18, pg 195, Vol. 19, pg 140, Vol. 20, pg 207
337. RG9 1C6 Vol. 19, pg 241, Vol. 20, pg 213
338. RG9 1C6 Vol. 20, pg 269 and RGU II C3A3 - 1867, pg 54
339. RG9 1C6 Vol. 19, pg 386 and Vol. 20, pg 253
340. RG9 1C6 Vol. 20, pg 303 and RGU II C3A3 - 1867, pg 54
341. RGU II C3A3 - 1867, pg 17
342. RG9 1C6 Vol. 19, pg 385 and Vol. 20, pg 252
343. RG9 1C6, Vol. 19, pg 307 and RGU II C3A3 - 1863, pg 54
344. RG9 1C6, Vol. 19, pg 396 and RGU II C3A3 - 1863, pg 56
345. RG9 1C6, Vol. 20, pg 187 and RGU II C3A3 - 1867, pg 68
346. RG9 1C6, Vol. 20, pg 188 and RGU II C3A3 - 1867, pg 68
347. RG9 1C6, Vol. 20, pg 188 and RGU II C3A3 - 1867, pg 68
348. RG9 II A5 Vol. 4, pgs 29, 87, 97 and Vol. 5, pgs 109, 110, 112-113
349. RG9 II A5 Vol. 4, pg 97 and Vol. 5, pgs 107-110, 112-113
350. RG9 II A5 Vol. 4, pgs 85-86 and Vol. 5, pgs 110, 112
351. RG9 II A5 Vol. 4, pg 97 and Vol. 5, pgs 109-112
352. RG9 II A5 Vol. 4, pg 88 and Vol. 5, pgs 112-113
353. RG9 1C1 Vol. 178 #226
354. 18 Victoria, Ch. 77, -1855, An Act to regulate the Militia of this province, and to repeal the Acts now in force for that purpose
355. 22 Victoria, Ch. 18, Sec. 15, -1859, An Act to amend and make permanent the laws relating to the Militia of this province
356 RGU II C3A3 - 1863, pg 59
357. RGU II C3A3 - 1866, pg 96
358 RGU IIC3A3 - 1863, pg 63
359. RGU II C3A3 - 1866, pg 99
360 RGU II C3A3 - 1866, pg 99
361 RGU II C3A3 - 1866, pg 100
362. RGU II C3A3 - 1863, pg 71
363 RGU II C3A3 - 1866, pg 102
364 RGU II C3A3 - 1865, pg 101
365. C. J. Purdon, The Snider-Enfield, Historical Arms Series No. 2, pg 2
366. 31 Victoria, (S. P. No. 35) 1867, pg 4
367. D. Owen, The Year of the Fenians, pg 78
368. RGU II C3A3 - 1866, pg 112
369. RGU II C3A3 - 1866, pg 113

ILLUSTRATION SOURCES

1. Private John Good; Courtesy of Myrtleville House Museum, Brantford, Ontario
2. Canadian Militia badge; Canadian Militia Badges – Pre 1914, D. Mazeas, pg 8
3. 38th Brant Battalion badge; Canadian Militia Badges – Pre 1914, D. Mazeas, pg 105
4. Grand Trunk Railway badge; Canadian Militia Badges – Pre 1914, D. Mazeas, pg 54
5. Map of Brant County; Courtesy of Ontario Genealogical Society: Brant County Branch, Brantford, Ontario
6. Hon. Dr. J. Y. Bown; Brantford Courier, 60th Anniversary & Old Boys Number, Dec 1899, pg 12, Courtesy of Brant County Museum & Archives, Brantford, Ontario
7. Hon. David Christie, Courtesy of National Archives of Canada, Ottawa, Ontario, Picture #PA26605
8. Hon. E. B. Wood; Courtesy of National Archives of Canada, Ottawa, Ontario, Picture #PA28640
9. Lt. Col. C. S. Perley; The Early Political and Military History of Burford, R. C. Muir, pg 281
10. Lt. Col. James Wilkes; Courtesy of Brant County Museum & Archives, Brantford, Ontario, #673
11. Locomotive "Milwaukee"; Courtesy of National Archives of Canada, Ottawa, Ontario, Picture #C2611
12. Canadian Volunteer Militia on Parade, 1866; Courtesy of Archives of Ontario, Toronto, Ontario #C286-1-0-6-1
13. Paris Junction, 1860s; Courtesy of Paris Museum and Historical Society, Paris, Ontario
14. Militia Canteen at Fort Erie, 1866; Troublous Times in Canada, J. Macdonald, pg 87
15. Fenian Raid, Irish Bond; Troublous Times in Canada, J. Macdonald
16. Town of Paris; Courtesy of Paris Public Library Board, Paris, Ontario, E7-b, #1407
17. Market Square, Brantford; Courtesy of Brant County Museum & Archives, Brantford, Ontario, #262
18. Canadian Volunteer Militia Officers, 1866; Courtesy of Archives of Ontario, Toronto, Ontario, #C286-1-0-6-3.1
19. Brantford Jail & Court House; Brant County History, Vol. II, Jean Waldie, pg 14
20. Chapel of the Delaware, Tuscarora; Courtesy of Mr. Part Peters, Tuscarora Township, Ontario
21. Paris Town Hall; Courtesy of Paris Public Library Board, Paris, Ontario
22. Captain William Patton; Courtesy of County of Brant, Burford, Ontario
23. Captain Andrew H. Baird; Courtesy of County of Brant, Burford, Ontario
24. Captain Hiram Dickie; Courtesy of the collection of Rick Shaver, Brantford, Ontario
25. Commercial Hotel; Courtesy of Brant County Museum & Archives, Brantford, Ontario, #1201
26. Kerby House, Brantford; Courtesy of Wayne Hunter, Brantford, Ontario
27. Captain William Grant; Brantford Expositor Souvenir Old Boys Reunion, Dec 1899, pg 51 Courtesy of Brant County Museum & Archives, Brantford, Ontario
28. Lieut. J. J. Inglis; Brantford Expositor, 25th Anniversary Edition, Dec 1902, Courtesy of Brant County Museum & Archives, Brantford, Ontario
29. Buck Stove Works, Brantford; Courtesy of Brant County Museum & Archives, Brantford, Ontario, #248
30. David Spence; Courtesy of the collection of Rick Shaver, Brantford, Ontario
31. Captain Henry Lemmon; Brantford Courier, 60th Anniversary & Old Boys Number, Dec 1899, pg 31, Courtesy of Brant County Museum & Archives, Brantford, Ontario
32. Lieutenant John Ballachey; Courtesy of the collection of Rick Shaver, Brantford, Ontario
33. Captain Allan W. Ellis; The Early Political and Military History of Burford, R. C. Muir, pg 367
34. Mount Pleasant Drill Shed; Courtesy of Mrs. Pat Phelps, Mount Pleasant, Ontario
35. Corporal William Vivian; Courtesy of William Vivian, Orange Park, Florida, U.S.A.
36. Hearns Hall, Burford; Courtesy of Mrs. Brock Miller, Burford, Ontario
37. Captain Edmund Yeigh; The Early Political and Military History of Burford, R. C. Muir, pg 363
38. Stephen Wetmore and Rory Johnston; The Early Political and Military History of Burford, R. C. Muir, pg 363
39. Burford Drill Shed; Courtesy of Mr. Clayton Barker, Brantford, Ontario
40. Loney & Kirklands store, Burford; Courtesy of Mrs. Brock Miller, Burford, Ontario
41. Cornet Thomas Lloyd-Jones; Brantford Expositor, Christmas edition 1892, pg 6, Courtesy of Brant County Museum & Archives, Brantford, Ontario
42. Captain William John Simcoe Kerr; Courtesy of Brant County Museum & Archives, Brantford, Ontario, #1326
43. Ensign John Buck; Courtesy of Woodland Cultural Centre, Brantford, Ontario
44. Captain Matthew Whiting; Courtesy of County of Brant, Burford, Ontario
45. Lt. Col. William Patton; Brantford Courier, 60th Anniversary & Old Boys Number, Dec 1899, pg 19, Courtesy of Brant County Museum & Archives, Brantford, Ontario
46. Camp at Thorold, 1866; From a watercolour by Alexander Von Erichsen. Courtesy of Fort Erie Museum, Fort Erie, Ontario
47. Alexandra Park Drill Shed, Brantford; Courtesy of Brant County Museum & Archives, Brantford, Ontario, #174
48. Canadian General Service Medal, Fenian Raid; Courtesy of Jeffrey Hoare Auctions, London, Ontario
49. Location Certificate; Courtesy of the collection of Rick Shaver, Brantford, Ontario
50. Pattern 1858 Enfield rifle; The Snider-Enfield, Historical Arms Series No. 2, Museum Restoration Service, Bloomfield, Ontario
51. Pre 1866 Uniform; Courtesy of the collection of Rick Shaver, Brantford, Ontario
52. Uniformed soldier of the 38th Battalion; Courtesy of the collection of Rick Shaver, Brantford, Ontario

BIBLIOGRAPHY

Government Document Sources

National Archives of Canada

RG9	Record Group 9, Military documents
RG9 1C1	Adjutant General's Office Correspondence, United Canada
RG9 1C3	Volunteer Militia Pay lists
RG9 1C6	Register of Officers, 1846-1869
RG9 II A5	Fenian Raid Medal Registers
RG9 II F6	Volunteer Militia Paylists
RGU II C3A3	Annual Volunteer Militia Lists

National Library of Canada

__Victoria (S. P. No. __,) Example: "31 Victoria (S. P. No. 35) - 1868" means in the 31st year of the reign of Queen Victoria, Sessional Paper number 35, year 1868. These documents can also be found in any university library with a good government documents section.

__Victoria, Ch. __, Sec.__ Example: "22 Victoria, Chapter 18, Section 15 - 1859. These documents contain Militia Acts or sections of Militia Acts within the Statutes passed by the Canadian parliament.

General Sources

Arnold S. and French T.; Custer's Forgotten Friend - The Life of W. W. Cooke, Adjutant, Seventh U. S. Cavalry

Barnard W. T., Lt. Col.; The Queen's Own Rifles of Canada, T. H. Best Printing Co., Don Mills, 1960

Brant County Council Minutes, June 21, 28, December 19, 1866

Brantford Courier, The; June 9, 1866; December 18, 1899 60th Anniversary Edition

Brantford Expositor, The; Brantford Public Library, Aug 8, 12, 1856; June 1, 1858; Jan 13, May 11, 1860; Aug 23, Sept 5, Oct 11, Nov 1, 1861; Jan 23, Feb 27, Mar 6, July 3, Sept 4, 1863; Dec 30, 1864; Jan 13, 20, 27, Feb 17, 24, Mar 31, Apr 7, 14, 1865; Jan 5, Feb 2, Mar 5, 9, 16, 23, 30, Apr 6, May 11, 25, June 1, 15, 22, July 20, 27, Aug 10, 24, Sept 7, 8, 14, 21, 28, Oct 5, 12, 19, 26, 30, 1866; Jan 18, Feb 1, 1867

Brantford Council Minutes; Jan 27, 1862; Jan 8, Mar 12, 26, June 1, July 23, Sept 17, 20, Nov 26, 1866

Sutherland, James; County of Brant Gazetteer and Directory for 1869-70, Hunter, Rose and Co., Toronto 1869

Dumfries Reformer, The; Cambridge Public Library, June 6, 1866

Galt Recorder, The; Cambridge Public Library, June 8, Sept 7, 1866

Guelph Mercury, The; Guelph Public Library, June 7, 1866

Grand River Sachem, The; June 20, 27, 1866

Hamilton Evening Times, The; Hamilton Public Library, Mar 10, June 2, 1866

Hamilton Spectator, The; Hamilton Public Library, Mar 10, 17, 1866

London Free Press, The; London Public Library, Mar 9, 31, June 1, 2, 4, 1866

London Public Library; Scrapbook, Vol 6 pg 73; Vol 7 pg 22

Macdonald John A., Capt.; Troublous Times in Canada, W. S. Johnston & Co., 1910

Montour, Enos T.; The Feathered U. E. L., 1973

Morton, Desmond; A Military History of Canada, Hurtig Publishers, Edmonton, 1985

Muir, R. C.; The Early Political and Military History of Burford, Hurley Printing, Brantford 1913

Mazeas, Daniel; Canadian Militia Badges - Pre 1914

Nelles, W. H., Lieut./Adjutant; Dufferin Rifles Standing Orders, Brantford, 1886

Norfolk Reformer; Simcoe Public Library, June 7, 14, 28, 1866

Oakland Council Minutes; June 18, 25, 1866

Owen, David; The Year of the Fenians, The Western New York Institute, 1990

Oxford County Scrapbook; London Public Library, Vol. 1 pg 43

Oxford Historical Item #32; Woodstock Public Library

Paris Council Minutes; Dec 17, 1855; Nov 3, 1856; Apr 6, 1857; Dec 23, 1861; Aug 31, Sept 3, 1866

Purdon, Charles J.; The Snider-Enfield, Historical Arms Series No. 2, Museum Restoration Service, Bloomfield, Ont.

Paris Review; Paris Public Library, April 30, 1896

Paris Star; Paris Public Library, Mar 8, 1865, June 22, 1866, Nov 20, 1867

Quealey, C. S. B.; The Fenian Invasion of Canada West, June 1, 2, 1866; Ontario Historical Society

Reville, F. D.; History of the County of Brant, Vol. I and Vol. II, Hurley Printing, Brantford, 1920

Sarnia Observer; The Sarnia Public Library, Oct 28, Nov 4, 1864; Jan 13, 20, Feb 17, Mar 17, 31, Apr 7, 14, 21, 28, May 5, 1865

Smith, Donald A.; At the Forks of the Grand, Vol. I. and Vol. II, Walker Press, Paris, 1982

Standing Orders of the 38th Battalion, The Dufferin Rifles of Canada; Toronto Reference Library, Watt & Shenston, 1886

Stanley, George F. G.; Canada's Soldiers, The Military History of an Unmilitary People, Macmillan of Canada, Toronto, 1974

Toronto Daily Globe, The; Hamilton Public Library, June 1, 6, 1866

Warner and Beers; The History of Brant County, Warner & Beers Co., 188

INDEX